IMAGES
of Wales

GRANGETOWN

Grange Farm standing alone in 1890 before the library or Stockland Street was built. To the right can be seen the backs of houses in Penhevad Street. Stockland Street was built in 1892.

IMAGES
of Wales

GRANGETOWN

Compiled by
Barbara Jones

TEMPUS

First published 1996, reprinted 2000
Copyright © Barbara Jones, 1996

Tempus Publishing Limited
The Mill, Brimscombe Port
Stroud, Gloucestershire GL5 2QG

ISBN 0 7524 0383 4

Typesetting and origination by
Tempus Publishing Limited
Printed in Great Britain by
Midway Clark Printing, Wiltshire

The masonry works of E. Turner & Sons Ltd in 1929. For years dressed stone had been sent in large quantities from here to many parts of Wales and England: as far north as Newcastle and east as far as Colchester. The workshop was replete with the most efficient electrically-driven machinery. An overhead gantry traversed the length of the works and transferred blocks of up to 12 tons to the diamond-saw moulding machines or for loading onto trucks. There was accomodation for 100 stone carvers, known in the building trade as banker masons.

Contents

Home Office pathologist, Professor Bernard Knight (b. 1931) lived at 118 Paget Street, and was educated at Herbert Thompson School, Ely, and St Illtyd's School. He studied at the Welsh National School of Medicine, Cardiff and Gray's Inn, London, before becoming a Medical Captain in the Royal Army Medical Corps with whom he spent three years on active service in Malaya (1956-1959). Before returning to Cardiff where he is now based at the Royal Infirmary, Professor Knight was president of many forensic and medical societies and lectured in Forensic Medicine at Whitechapel Hospital in London. He is also the author of several medical textbooks, crime novels, two Welsh historical novels and scripts for radio and television drama.

Foreword

For several reasons, I am pleased to have the opportunity to commend this book on Grangetown.

Firstly, it is a welcome addition to the growing number of books on the recent history of Cardiff, no doubt symptomatic of increasing nostalgia for former times.

Modern development is erasing old landmarks and imposing a uniformity on our cities that sometimes makes it difficult to tell parts of Cardiff from a score of other cities.

The other reason is that but for 'Grange', I wouldn't exist, as my parents met there, lived there and I was born there! My grandfather, Frederick Lawes, was an engineer in the Mount Stuart Dry Dock and lived in Paget Street, right opposite St Paul's Church. My father was the church organist there from the twenties until 1945 and met my mother as a member of the congregation. Though we moved to Fairwater in 1933, I was a choirboy at St Paul's all through the war. I had little choice, as my father was the choirmaster!

I still have vivid memories of 'Grange', such as the day war broke out. I remember Dyfrig, the son of Canon Lewis at St Paul's, wiring radio speakers into the church on 3 September 1939 so that we could all hear the momentous broadcast by Neville Chamberlain at 11 o'clock telling us that war had started. The beautiful summer evening before Dunkirk is still clear in my mind, with anxious parishioners talking it through on the pavement in Paget Street. The air-raid sirens, the shelters and the 'ack-ack' guns were all part of life in Grange in those days.

The numerous photographs and the painstaking research that has gone into this book bring back so many recollections of a district that was one of the pillars of Cardiff's industrial past, when most people in Grangetown had some connection with 'The Docks', supporting what at the turn of the century, was the busiest port in the world.

Professor Bernard Knight CBE

THE SPIRIT OF GRANGETOWN

BY MILLIE

My footsteps returned to the Grange today,
  The landmarks I sought had vanished away.
Regretfully, I reminisced
  For the Grangetown I knew was not like this.

Then all of a sudden the scene changed,
  T'was as if the days of old remained,
People I'd known to my surprise
  Re-enacted their lives before my eyes.

The shops around me began to unfold
  And carried on business just as of old.
Arkle the post office opened his door
  To sell his halfpenny stamps once more.

For a shilling a week, marked on a card,
  Pryce Griffiths sold his shoes
For the times were hard.
  Paisley, the draper, down on the square,
Poppy Whiteing also was there.
  Bann, the butcher, doing well,
And Stones, the grocer, so they tell.

Dolly Cazananve made her start
  Delivering milk with her small handcart.
Jimmy Nurse the insurance, cycling around.
  Harry Parsons, too, I found.

By the Lord Windsor, always at hand,
  Billy, the bookie, furtively stands.
Now the Salvation Army band comes,
  With big Mr. Norton playing the drums.
For it's Monday night and off we go
  To see the magic lantern show,
With slides designed to make us think
  About the folly of demon drink.

They were dancing the New Year in on the square,
  All of the streets were gathering there.
And as they sang the Auld Lang Syne,
  Somebody linked their arm in mine.
With tears of joy, I found at last
  The spirit I sought of Grangetown past.

With youth renewed I wandered at will
  Over the tide fields and the red hills.
Past the Red House to the old subway,
  Searched for the penny toll to pay.

I child again, I stood on the deck
  Of the Old Louisa's creaking wreck,
The children were playing on the stones
  And the men were rowing their little boats home.

Slowly back to the Marl I made my way,
  Pausing to watch The Albions play,
For baseball was ever
  The match of our day.

As I walked along the Old Docks Road,
  A cart on the tip emptied its load,
I joined in the search with the waiting boys
  Eager to dig in the dirt for the coins.

The sea had reclaimed its land once more
  It arose to the Boat House dirt pavement shore.
Old Bill the Boatman hurried by
  Tipping his cap as he caught my eye.

Finally to the canal we came
  And dived off the James Street Bridge again.
With jolly rivalry we boast,
  Jumping the logs at the Timber Float.

Finding myself alone once more,
  I made my way past the John Bull store,
Before I travelled very far,
  I came to Longstaffs Penny Bazaar.

There at the top of Paget Street
  Once again I stopped to greet,
The folk that kept a fresh fish stall,
  Known to us all as The Hole in the Wall.

We queued for the twopenny rush up the Nin,
  Alfalfa, Ken Maynard, Rin Tin Tin.
We cheered or booed as the battle raged
  And whistled and called when the cameras failed.
When the pictures were over, out we came,
  I was Tonto, you were Tom Mix all over again.

For my childhood home I began to yearn,
  A consuming need within me burned.
Instinctively my footsteps turned
  With nostalgic heart I hurried along
But the house I knew as home was gone,
  And where the terraced street had been
All that remained was a plot of green.

I looked at my hands,
  They were wrinkled and old,
Suddenly, I felt quite cold,
  For the Spirit of Grangetown that used to be
Only exists in my memory.

Introduction

by Sir James Lyons KCSG, OStJ, JP

Without doubt, Grangetown is an important part of Cardiff. Its citizens are considered most friendly, hospitable and helpful, with tremendous community spirit. It is safe to say they meet up in all parts of the globe and the welcome and acknowledgement to one another is great.

Now what shall I say to start my contribution? Well, I was born in Stockland Street of Cardiff-born parents in 1910. My mother became a local midwife who was exceedingly well-known and sought after. In those days babies were born 'at home' and very rarely was a doctor present. The nurse then looked after the mother and child (some did have twins) for fourteen days of washing, feeding and counselling.

I went to St Patrick's School and later to Ninian Park and then passed the entrance examination for Howard Gardens Grammar School. At that time St Illtyd's had not opened.

I played rugby, baseball (first division Canton BC) and many was the time I was caught swimming in the Taff near Sophia Gardens, the Glamorgan Canal off James Street (diving from the pilot boats) and the timber ponds situated near Tresilian Terrace and Dumballs Road. Often, we were chased by the Docks Police.

Baseball was played on the Marl, Bendix Field or Sevenoaks Park. Not the most healthy of spots. One always needed a good hot bath at home. I wonder how many can remember the American warship docking in Cardiff and its crew deciding to challenge the Grange Albions to a game of American baseball. I feel sure of the shock and amazement of the Americans when they were well beaten. Many of the Grange team were offered appointments to play in America but I cannot recall anyone going.

Grangetown was well supplied with churches and chapels: St Paul's in Paget Street, St Samson's in Pentre Street and St Barnabas' in Court Road, all Church of England and the Ebenezer, Presbyterian, Congregational, Methodist, Salvation Army and Roman Catholic chapels.

The 'young bloods' created some religious rivalry especially at Whit Sunday treat-time and Corpus Christi processions. From such an event I met my late wife, Doreen Fogg.

Grangetown had its share of clubs: the Conservatives in Corporation Road, the Catholic Club in Corporation Road, the Labour Club in Tudor Street, the Lindon in Clare Road (considered Liberal) and the Non Political Club in Penarth Road. There were also many renowned public houses which attracted many 'supporters'. Grange Gardens, meanwhile, was a delight with its well-kept lawns, flower beds, bowling-greens and tennis-courts, well controlled by 'Billy the Keeper'.

Outdoor meetings, especially at election times, were a great feature and always attracted many hundreds of people, and yes the soap-box was in use. The prime location was the junction of Corporation Road, Paget Street, Penarth Road and Havelock Place. Heckling and questions always caused great interest and excitement.

At this time coal-fires were the main form of heating for the average household. Only later did we get gas ovens and electricity. Before this, many Christmas cakes and sometimes 'the bird' were taken to the baker's for cooking. We were well supplied with bakers: Bruton's in Holmesdale Street (still there); Hollyman's in Corporation Road (sadly all killed in the blitz); Hall's in Paget Street; Squire's in Clare Road (still there); and Bowden's in Lucknow Street. We had quite a few coal merchants: O'Donovan's in Ferndale Street; Harris Boys, Taff Embankment; Cummings in Dorset Street and Bill Aplin whose brother was a furniture removal man in Warwick Place.

Most Grangetown men, were associated with the docks – Cardiff, Penarth and Barry being the greatest coal-exporting ports in the world. Ships in those days were driven by coal-fired boilers and coaling stations were established all over the world. Steel rails were shipped to India for the construction of their railways. The rails were manufactured at the Dowlais Works at East Moors. We imported food of all kinds, fruit from South America, South Africa, and later Israel, meat from the Argentine and New Zealand, timber from Sweden and Norway.

Probably the most exciting day of my life was being selected as Lord Mayor of Cardiff in May 1968. During my year in office I was fortunate to meet most members of the Royal Family.

Sir James Lyons, Rt. Hon. Lord Mayor of Cardiff, 1968-69. He is seen here with HM The Queen, HRH Prince Philip, HRH The Prince of Wales, on the occasion of their visit to the capital on 17 December that year. Also pictured with Sir James and Lady Doreen are, from left to right, in the back row: Sidney Tapper Jones, Judge Sir Mars Jones, Canon Trevor Driscoll, Elizabeth Lyons, and Colin Lyons.

One

Grange Farm: Early History

The great Cistercian abbey of Margam was founded in 1147 by Robert, earl of Gloucester, the lord of Glamorgan and illegitimate son of Henry I, when he granted his land at Margam to the 'white monks'. At some later date, between 1193 and 1218, Henry, Bishop of Llandaff, granted to Margam Abbey, lands on the moor to the west of the borough, lying between the mouth of the river Taff and the great Pill near the bishop's sheepfold forming part of his hamlet of Canton. The word 'pill' (in old English 'pyll') means a tidal creek and may derive from a British word for pool. At low tide the 'pill' is empty, filling with the incoming tide. On these, the Bishop's lands, the Abbey established a grange, variously termed in its deeds as 'Granga de Mora', 'Moregraunge' and 'Abbot's Grange'. The grange was an outpost of the Abbey and housed the monks while they farmed the land too far away for them to 'commute' every day. It is said that monks who were disobedient were sent here as part of their punishment. So began the grange of the 'Mora juxta Kaerdif' which gave the monks the opportunity to exploit the seamarshes between the Taff and the Ely rivers.

The ancient monastic tithebarn, it would appear, was granted by the first Gilbert de Clare (1243-95), who obtained in the year following his succession the earldom of Gloucester and the Lordship of Glamorgan. The house of Clare (after which one of Grangetown's principal thoroughfares is named) was one to be reckoned with, for the Clare ancestry could be traced to Count Godfrey, eldest of the extramarital sons of Richard the Fearless, Duke of Normandy. Fearless too was Gilbert's grandson and namesake, otherwise known as the 'Red Earl'. He was described as 'the most powerful subject in the Kingdom' and no one was more aware of this than the abbot and monks of Margam Abbey, who were deprived of their grange between 'Thaf and Ely' by 'Red Gilbert' in 1290. It was restored to them in 1328, however, after an inquisition by a grand jury. Gilbert de Clare's charter of confirmation describes the land as being 'all our moor which lies outside our new walda in Cardiff between the walda and the sea between the Taff and Ely rivers'. The Grange lands therefore lay in what was known as Leckwith Moors. Using modern points of reference the manor of the Grange seems to have extended from the foreshore on the south, up the river Ely to the railway, then roughly through St Patrick's School and back just south-west of Corporation Road to the Taff. In the extent of 1336, the monks are shown as holding 20 acres of arable at the 'sheepfold at the mora and 10 acres of meadow'.

In 1492, the Abbey leased its grange through Jasper Tudor, uncle of King Henry VII, to Griffith ap Meuric who also farmed the 'Grange of Luquyth' and pastured a hundred oxen and four hundred sheep on the, grasslands behind the sea-wall. In that year 7s 1d was paid for carting 17 loads of hay from Abbots Grange to the lords 'hayhouse within the town of Cardiff'.

Margam Abbey was suppressed by Henry VIII in 1537 following his order for the dissolution of the monasteries, and the 'Grange on the moor' was sold to Thomas Lewis of the Van (Caerphilly). Before the dissolution the Grange had been leased to Sir Roger Vaughan whose family had certain interests in Cardiff, but from 1518 onwards it was leased by the Abbey to a farmer, Lewis ap Richard, the last man to hold his land from Margam Abbey. His lease ran as follows: 'Unto all Christ's faithful to whom the present writing shall come, we John, Abbot of the Monastery of the Blessed Virgin of Margam and the convent of that place, greeting. Know ye that we have delivered to Lewis ap Richard esquire our grange near the town of Kaerdiff, commonly called More Grange until the end term of 90 years. Rendering £6

13s 4d sterling payable at the Feast of the Annunciation of the Blessed Virgin Mary and her Assumption by equal portions, four shillings annually to the Bishop of Llandaff, and two acres of hay a year to the Abbot. And the aforesaid Lewis will well and suitably repair and maintain and in good condition deliver up the aforesaid grange in houses, sea walls, weirs, ditches and fences. Given in our Chapter house of our Monastery aforesaid on 23rd March in this year of our lord 1517, and the ninth year of King Henry VIII'.

An official document dated 1547 relating to the Grange describes it as 'parcel of the lands of the late Monastery of Margam, suppressed by authority of Parliament' and the tenant Edward Llewelyn is significantly described as 'our lord the King's farmer there'. His rent was £6 13s 4d, interestingly the same annual rent received from Lewis ap Richard some thirty years earlier. It is significant that there was some depreciation in the state of the farm which is evident from the fact that by 1595 the rent was only 44s a year arising from 'one messuage, one barn, and one parcel of land, meadow and pasture called Le Graing de Moore, parcel of the lands of the late Monastery of Margam'.

Thomas Lewis of the Van died in 1595 leaving the lands at Grange to be passed on to a long line of male heirs. In 1638 'the manor lands called the Grange Marshes' contained 300 acres, each of a yearly value of four pence and were bounded by the higher lands of 'Pennarth' in the west, 'the Severne shore' on the south, and the river 'Tave' on the east and the common lands of Leckwith in the north. The eighteenth century saw the cessation of male heirs in the Lewis family. With no male heir left the Grange became absorbed into the Plymouth estate when the Lewis heiress married the earl of Plymouth. This is where the story of Peter Farr the present owner of Grange Farm begins. In 1836 Peter's great-great-grandparents, Thomas Morgan and his wife Mary were sent to Grange Farm from St Fagans where they were employed by the earl of Plymouth. The Grange land at that time extended as far as Grange Point (see map opposite) and supported both cattle and sheep. Thomas and Mary had six children, four boys and two girls. Thomas died in 1879, and Mary ran the farm until 1881 when she too died. On her death, the farm was taken over by her daughter Ann (born 1846) and her husband Sam Burford. Sam had come to Cardiff from Corfe in Somerset to find work at the docks. He went to sea for a time and his indentures classed him as a shipwright (ship's carpenter). Ann and Sam's son Thomas Henry Burford married Amelia Cook and their daughter Doris, born in 1909, inherited the farm when her parents died. Another daughter Lillian married Gilbert Farr. Doris Burford remembered her young days fondly, the house being the life and soul of Grangetown, 'Everyone used to visit the farm, it was the only house for miles. Life was good in those days, but hard work.' She would get up at four o'clock to start the milk round: in the early years with a horse and cart, and then later in a van.

Life revolved around the hearth and Doris's mother cooked for the family of five children using the oven of the big black range that took up the entire wall of what is now the lounge. In those days the floors were of flagstone and whole pigs were cut up on the pine table in the kitchen. The Burford family kept animals, ran the milk round (they used to sell milk straight from the shed) and later they had a coal round, that side of the business being managed by Doris's brother Frank. Doris Burford never married, and on her death Grange Farm passed to Lillian and Gilbert's son Peter. Today, there is still evidence of the early occupation in an archway which is now part of a window but was originally a doorway. Also remaining in the north wall of the building is a window showing medieval tracery.

Opposite: Walker's map from the 1840s shows just Grange Farm and its land which stretched south as far as Grange Point.

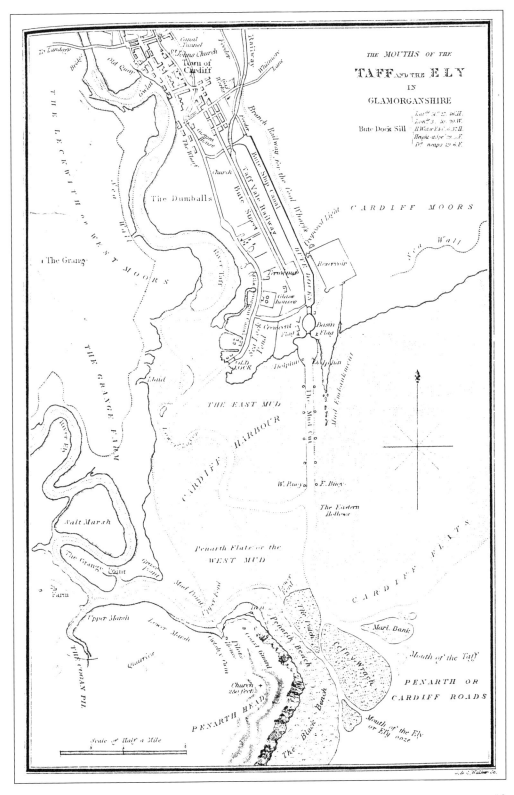

THE MOUTHS OF THE
TAFF AND THE ELY
IN
GLAMORGANSHIRE

IN LANDAFF PARISH.

LOT 21.

A CAPITAL TYTHE-FREE

GRAZING AND DAIRY FARM,

NEAR CARDIFF,

Called the GRANGE,

NOW IN THE OCCUPATION OF MRS. MARY JAMES;

CONSISTING OF

			A.	R.	P.	A.	R.	P.
A Farm-House, with Buildings and Garden - - -			0	1	20			
Ten Acres -			13	1	4			
Nine Acres -			11	1	30			
Eight Acres -			9	0	31			
Three Acres -			3	3	38			
Seven Acres -	Meadow and Pasture Lands within the		7	3	29			
Two Acres -	old Sea Wall		3	0	21			
Twenty-three Acres			30	0	.5			
Sixteen Acres -			18	2	37			
Eleven Acres -			13	1	25			
Sea Wall -			1	1	20			
Salt Marsh, about 50 Acres of which have been lately banked in - - - - - -	Pasture	178	1	2				
						291	0	22

This document dates from around 1812 and a Mrs Mary James was the tenant farmer at the time.

Opposite: Waring's 1869 map shows a developing Grangetown. There is now a rope works, iron works (which failed), a brick yard, a tannery and the gas works. The tannery was situated at Sevenoaks Park which is even today called 'The Tan' by the local residents.

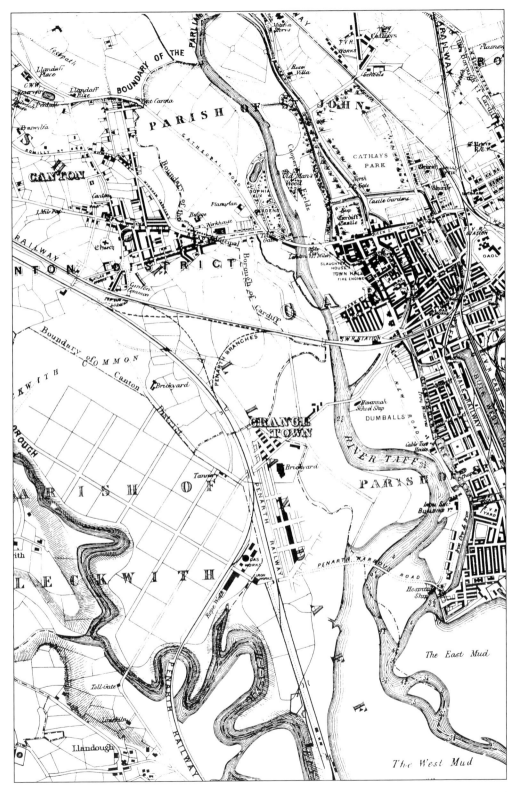

Thomas and Mary Morgan the great-great-grandparents of the present owner of Grange Farm.

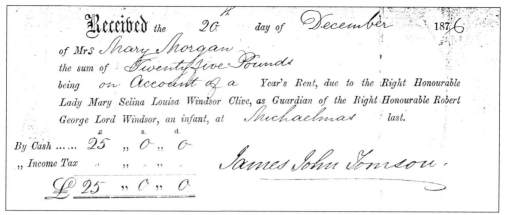

Received the 20th day of **December** 1876
of Mrs *Mary Morgan*
the sum of *Twenty five Pounds*
being *on Account of a* Year's Rent, due to the Right Honourable
Lady Mary Selina Louisa Windsor Clive, as Guardian of the Right Honourable Robert
George Lord Windsor, an infant, at *Michaelmas* last.

By Cash ...... 25 „ 0 „ 0
„ Income Tax „ „ „
£ 25 „ 0 „ 0

James John Jonson

Two receipts in the name of Mrs Mary Morgan. The one below, dated September 1880, was just a year before her death.

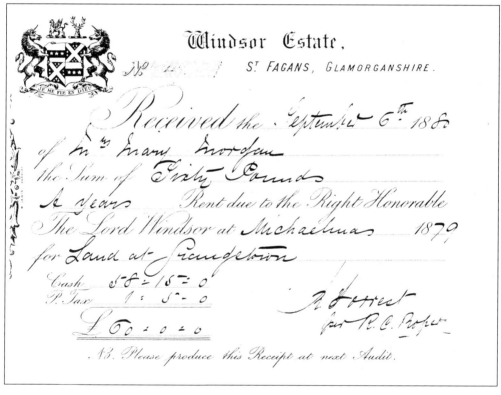

Windsor Estate,

Nº ST. FAGANS, GLAMORGANSHIRE.

Received the *September 6th 1880*
of *Mrs Mary Morgan*
the Sum of *Sixty Pounds*
A years Rent due to the *Right Honorable*
The Lord Windsor at Michaelmas 1879
for Land at Grangetown

Cash 58 : 15 : 0
P. Tax 1 : 5 : 0
£ 60 : 0 : 0

R Forrest
for R. C. Proper

N.B. Please produce this Receipt at next Audit.

This 1886 Ordnance Survey map shows how Grangetown had developed since 1869 (see page 15).

Grange Farm's dairy herd was grazed on the Marl. Every morning before setting off for school, Lillian Burford used to help collect the cows and bring them to the farmhouse for milking. On occasions, children would throw stones at the cows and chase her through the streets. The cows were sold in 1914 and, milk was then bought in. Lillian's father also kept shire horses and was a haulier with E. Turner & Sons. Doris Burford, Lillian's sister is well remembered by Grange folk on her milk round with horse and cart. People brought their jugs which Doris filled by ladle from the churns.

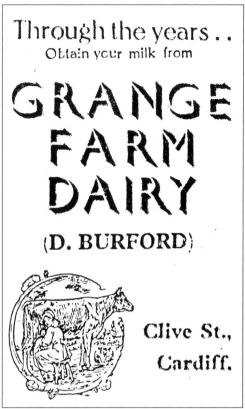

Through the years ..
Obtain your milk from

GRANGE FARM DAIRY

(D. BURFORD)

Clive St., Cardiff.

The Burford family outside Grange Farm in 1892. From left to right: William Burford, Elizabeth Burford, Albert Burford (sitting on the wall), his father and mother Sam and Ann Burford, their son Henry Burford, Mary Burford, Harriet, Eleanor and Sam.

Preparing for the milk round, Grange Farm, 1913.

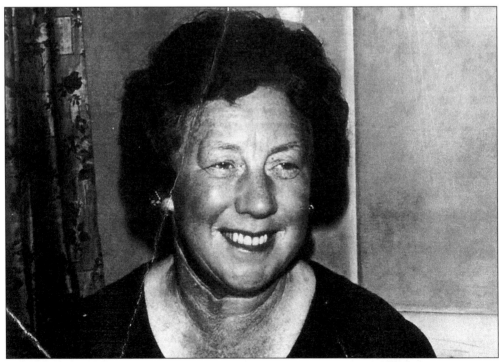

Doris Burford who ran Grange Farm for many years. Peter Farr, her nephew, came to live at Grange Farm in 1988. Doris died in 1993.

This window is set in the north-facing wall of Grange Farm and was hidden for centuries before being uncovered some years ago. With its Gothic tracery, it is almost certainly the remains of one of the original windows of the medieval building.

This medieval archway has been cleverly turned into a window, with the attractive stained glass appropriately depicting a monk. This was the original doorway of the ancient monastic tithe barn which stood on this site.

Peter Farr in the lounge of Grange Farm. He bears a striking likeness to his great-great-grandparents, Thomas and Mary Morgan. The Grange farmhouse became a Cadw grade II listed building on 19 May 1975. About 90 per cent of all listed buildings fall into this category which means they are of 'more than special interest.'

Two

Grangetown:
from the 1850s

Grangetown lies to the west of Cardiff and forms a clearly defined area bounded by the Taff to the east, the sea to the south, Canton to the north and the River Ely to the west. In 1850 the Marquis of Bute and the Hon. Robert Clive agreed to construct a road, from St Mary Street in Cardiff to Penarth with bridges across the Taff and Ely at the joint expense of the Bute and Windsor estates. The road was to be used without any charge by either party exept for a toll, collected at the Ely bridge by the Bute estate which was to be responsible for the repair of the road. It was reported by the Bute solicitors in 1868 that existing bridges over the Taff and Ely, had become so dilapidated that their reconstruction must be commenced without any further delay. The bridges were rebuilt between 1868 and 1871 at a joint cost to the two estates of £12,732. So the effort of the Bute and Windsor estates provided a link with central Cardiff along the present Penarth Road. This preceded building development. It does not seem to have been planned deliberately but obviously a link with Cardiff was necessary for the creation of the suburb of Grangetown. The Penarth Dock, Harbour and Railway Company sought a link by road with the docks at Cardiff and came to an agreement in 1866 with the Bute and Windsor estates. The company contributed £1,000 and the price of the land towards the road. A bridge was built across the Taff, south of the Clarence Bridge which replaced it in 1890 (see photograph on page 26). This was an important development for a large number of Grangetown residents were employed at the docks. Grangetown at this time was a 'walking' suburb. The Cardiff Tramway Company had crossed the Taff in 1877 but only served Canton. Grangetown, itself, was served by the Cardiff District and Penarth Harbour Tramway which began operating in 1881. The building development of Grangetown was made possible by an Estate Act obtained in 1857 permitting Lady Windsor and the trustees to sell land or raise money to improve the estate. Lady Windsor made hopeful reference to the 'new town we may now expect to see spring up on the Grange'. Immediate steps were taken to make this possible by raising mortgages on farms in the surrounding area, under the 1857 Estate Act. Contracts were put out for roads and drainage at Grangetown and Penarth. By June 1865 £30,508 12s 2d had been spent on estate improvements. Between 1857 and 1873 the Windsor estate invested heavily in roads and drainage at Grangetown. The expenditure was £14,000 up to 1860, £400 to 1869 and around £3,400 after that date. As a result of this, two groups of streets in upper and lower Grange were drained by the most efficient sewage system in Cardiff.

Up to 1875 the development at Grangetown was probably just breaking even but such a situation was in fact expected in the initial stages. However, it seems that the development at Grangetown had been misjudged or at least mistimed. The figures for house plans approved in Cardiff suggest that the development coincided with a trough in house building. The estate surveyor commented in 1860: 'at present things are very languid at Cardiff generally as well as Penarth and Grange'. By 1871 it was pointed out that the scheme had remained comparatively stationary for some seven or eight years. More than the unfortunate timing, it is possible that the basis of the scheme was misjudged. Grangetown was initially planned as an industrial suburb and not as the commuting suburb it eventually became. In 1862 the estate agents wanting to see local industrial establishments giving employment to numbers of men pinned their hopes on the ironworks. The theory behind this was that Cardiff, but more especially Grange, would not become permanantly prosperous without them. The ironworks in fact was never a success. Although a road was built to the site in 1864 the scheme was abandoned. The ironworks was eventually built but by 1880 it had passed from hand to hand and had been closed for most of its existence. It restarted as the Penarth Iron and Steel Company but had failed again by 1881.

Another misjudgement was the importance attached to avoiding local rates and to remaining outside any local board of health. The fact that Grangetown was outside the Canton and Cardiff local boards was regarded as being beneficial to the development, and in 1859 was attraction for speculative builders, but by 1875 it was considered a disadvantage because of the expense to the estate of providing street sewers which elsewhere were provided by the local board out of the rates. In 1875 the sewers were taken over by the local board of health when Grangetown (together with Canton) was incorporated into the borough of Cardiff.

The result of the Windsor estate development was a respectable working-class suburb with some lower middle-class houses near the church and larger houses facing the sea. In 1862 there had been 132 houses in Grange with a population of 660, but a writer describing the district as it was about 1880 says: 'There were two distinct villages known as Upper and Lower Grangetown each consisting of about half a dozen streets and separated from the town of Cardiff by at least a mile of open country. Penarth Road, the main road, was flanked with hedgerows on either side.' An old newspaper of 1901 records the 'thickly populated portion of Grangetown lying between Bromsgrove Street and Penarth Road. Grange is described as 'a vast suburb of the Welsh Metropolis with a population of 17,000 souls.' This expansion was typical of the growth of Cardiff itself.

By the time old Grangetown was really established, the majority of the locals worked at the nearby Cardiff Docks, many men being coaltrimmers, a job now defunct. Other workers were employed at the numerous dairies, bakehouses, or builder's yards. The railway also provided employment. The first electric tramcar came into Grangetown in 1902 running along Corporation Road and also Clare Road and people could travel anywhere in the city for one penny. Another route along Penarth Road and Clive Street arrived a year or so later. The tramcars continued to run in Grangetown until 1942 when trolley-buses took over on the Corporation Road route. Motor-buses had already come into operation on the Penarth Road-Clive Street run in 1936.

Holmesdale Street is claimed by many local people to be the heart of Grangetown. This end of Grangetown became known as Lower Grange while the Saltmead end became Upper Grange. According to an old Cardiff records book dated 1905, Saltmead is listed as 'low land over which the sea flows at every high tide'. Gillards Field now Sevenoaks Park, was one such place where water would collect not from the sea but from rainfall. Saltmead was an area inside the Cardiff Central to Grangetown railway line, Virgil Street, Sloper Road, Penarth Road, and Taffs Mead Embankment. A few street names changed when Saltmead became Upper Grange. Saltmead Road became Stafford Road, Taffs Mead Place became Merches Place and Staughton Street is now Jubilee Street. Many different races settled in Saltmead. Men gambled on the street corners, police walked around the area in pairs, some households kept donkeys in their back kitchens and pigs in their passages (according to a history of Saltmead by Colin Weston). The roads were empty in the early days apart from the horses and carts of the milkmen, coalmen and the local builders. (See the volume on Canton, also published in The Archive Photographs Series, by the late Bryan Jones, which contains much complementary information).

A drawing of the flood in Ludlow Street showing the gates of the Wesleyan Chapel. Grange was a saltmarsh i.e. land liable to be overflowed by the sea. How true this proved to be on Wednesday, 17 October 1883. On that night there was a particularly high tide. The water burst through the sea-dyke opposite Kent Street, catching people unawares, and flowed through the streets reaching a height of 5 ft. Mr Sam Thomas the hairdresser provided the above sketch of the flood and tells this story: 'There was a Harvest Thanksgiving Service in the Wesleyan Chapel and the Minister was preaching when a man rushed in shouting "The Flood! The Flood is coming!" The preacher at once comforted his people and told them to be brave and to have courage – then fainted.' There was also a Harvest Service in the Iron Room that night and worshippers had to be rescued and escorted home in Sam Norton's 'pram' and other available boats.

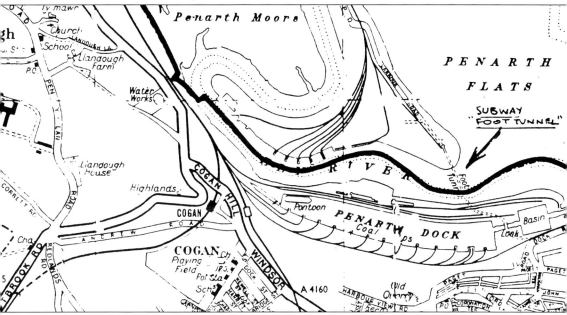

To avoid a very long detour, a subway – marked 'foot tunnel' on the above map – was constructed beneath the River Ely, from the Southern extremity of Ferry Road to the lock-gate platform of Penarth Dock. It was the only river tunnel in Cardiff. Construction, rather like the London 'Tubes', was of bolted iron segments, with lights at regular intervals. The hard reflecting materials endowed it with a strong characteristic reverberating echo – often exploited by the young. Approaching footsteps could be heard from one end to the other, rather fearfully. A toll of one penny was levied. For the impecunious, it was a cheap way of getting to the seaside.

The Taff Vale Railway (TVR) Company built this bridge over the River Taff in the middle of the nineteenth century in order to get its work force to the docks more quickly. When, after a number of years, the company decided to impose a toll on the users local people vehemently objected. This led to the council's decision to build the Clarence Road and James Street swing-bridges. The TVR Bridge was closed and dismantled some time between 1892 and 1895. The Clarence Road Bridge was built further along the river in 1889-90.

The famous 'Hotel de Marl', 1882. When the Welsh Sunday Closing Act was passed in 1881 it stopped the working man having a drink on Sundays. So men in Grangetown opened up their own drinking booths on the Marl. They circumnavigated the law by giving the drink away free but between two burly dockers lay a greasy cap which accepted 'donations' for the drink taken by the customers. The booths had their own names: Hotel de Boilermakers, Hotel de Coalminers and a 'cosmopolitan' one – Hotel de Marl. When the drink ran low, for the booths did a roaring trade much to the disgust of the local chapel folk, a lady was despatched with an empty pram to purchase a new barrel from a local 'shebeen' [an illicit liquor shop]. Eventually Conservative, Liberal, non political, and later Labour clubs emerged to slake the people's thirst on Sundays.

Opposite: On 31 May 1889 the Mayor, Alderman David Jones, and members of the Grangetown Bridges Committee met to inspect the construction of the Grangetown Bridge later to be called the Clarence Road Bridge.

The Penarth ferry over the River Ely was from 1866 the terminus of Penarth Harbour Road. This road crossed the canal lock on a wooden swing-bridge, passed along a short road in front of the *Hamadryad* hospital ship, crossed the River Taff on a wooden trestle bridge with a central swing span to the point where Avondale and Ferry Road meet, then ran along the latter to the ferry at the south end of the peninsular between the two rivers. Solomon Andrews ran a horse-bus from Stuart Street along this route to connect with the ferry. Between 1885 and 1888 three terraces of existing houses in Ferry Road, between Clive and Kent streets, were built: Andrews Terrace, Fair View and Sea View. The decision of the Taff Vale Railway Company, who owned the old road and bridge, to charge tolls on users in 1886 led the council to build a new swing-bridge 350 yards north of the original structure. This siting enabled the council to open up a direct communication between James Street and Penarth Road by means of a swing-bridge across the canal and the construction of the present Clarence, Avondale and Corporation roads. To the Cardiff residents the bridge was the eighth wonder of the world: it measured 464 ft in length, the swinging portion was 190 ft and was a considerable engineering achievement of the age. It was rarely opened, and mostly on Sunday mornings to allow a dredger to work near the Penarth Road Bridge where a pumping station maintained the level of water in the timber ponds. These were drained by 1937 and the land was reclaimed for extension northwards of Curran's engineering works for the rearmament drive. In 1941 Parliament relieved the the City Council of its legal obligation (dating from 1887) to operate it as a swing-bridge. Above, the new Clarence Bridge is shown being opened on 17 September 1890, amidst great ceremony, by the Duke of Clarence and Avondale. The old bridge, meanwhile, remained in use until *c.* 1898.

It would be interesting to know what PC William Price wrote in his notebook on the day this accident occurred on the Clarence Bridge.

This bonfire at Grangetown, like hundreds of others all over the country, was lit to celebrate Queen Victoria's Diamond Jubilee on 22 June 1897. It was a grand imperial festival. The Queen was 78 and so suffered from rheumatism that the short service at St Paul's Cathedral in London was held outside the building to avoid carrying her up the steps in a wheelchair.

Nurse Milford was the local midwife in the early 1900s. She worked from home at 23 Ludlow Street and died aged 73 in 1935. Over the years she brought thousands of infants into the world including a number of gypsy babies from the camp on the area known as the 'Red Hills', adjoining the Marl. Nurse Milford was delivering babies until six weeks before she died.

The bandstand in Grange Gardens (1895) was the first one to be erected in a Cardiff park. To the right in the background is the war memorial. Sadly this bandstand has long since vanished as have so many other attractive features of Grangetown.

This was how Clive Street looked in 1908. The right of the photograph shows a confectionery shop on the corner of Bromsgrove Street.

The Samuel family became well-known in Cardiff between 1907 and 1915 for presenting fountains in memory of their parents and Louis, their elder brother. Louis, who ran a furniture business on the in The Hayes, became Cardiff's first Jewish JP in 1896. The memorial to Louis Samuel was unveiled in Grange Gardens on 13 July 1909.

Penarth Road. This is the junction with Havelock Place, Clare Road, Corporation Road, and Paget Street. Turner's office buildings stood on the corner of Havelock Place and Havelock Lane, just to the left, out of the picture. The chapel on the corner of Clare Road was demolished after it was gutted by fire. A supermarket was built on the site in 1973.

In 1902 this open-top tram was one of twenty built by Dick Kerr. It cost £540 and ran on the Clare Road Depot-St Mary Street-Clarence Road route. After much controversy as to whether the trolley-bus system would be viable in Cardiff it was finally decided to go ahead and introduce this form of transport. The worst section between Wood Street and Clarence Road via Grangetown was selected for the first conversion. The inauguration ceremony took place in March 1942 and the trolley-bus service operated for almost thirty years.

In 1865 horse-buses were running from Queen Street to Pier Head. By 1902 transport was being revolutionised by the introduction of the electric tram. The first motor-bus was introduced in 1920 but the last tramcars were not withdrawn until 1950.

Grangetown railway station, seen from Penarth Road in the early years of the century. Older readers will remember roaring coal-fires in the waiting rooms during the winter months.

These gentlemen were members of the Cork Club and posed for their photograph outside the London Style Inn in Lucknow Street on 14 July 1919 before their annual picnic. The London Style pub was probably built in 1879 as the date of the first transfer was 3 November that year. It has now been demolished.

Florence Hilda Lyons (*née* Driscoll) from Mardy Street, who was the local midwife in the 1920s. In those days of the Poor Law when there was no National Health Service, the nurse attended for fourteen days and at the end received the princely sum of ten shillings. A doctor would attend for two shillings, and a visit to the surgery cost one shilling. Dr Evans in Corporation Road was the local doctor at the time. Hilda Lyons was the mother of Sir James Lyons who became Lord Mayor of Cardiff in 1968 (see Foreword).

Mr and Mrs Crockford of Ludlow Street were a typical fashionable young couple of the day as illustrated by this photograph from the mid-1920s.

The Silver Jubilee of King George V and Queen Mary was celebrated in fine style by the residents of Oakley Street in 1935. It was just two years later that people were celebrating with street parties once again. This time the occasion was the coronation of the new king, George VI and Queen Elizabeth. Below, the ladies who organised the party in Warwick Street pose for their photograph.

Olive Guppy lived in Stafford Road and from an early age showed great talent as a musician on piano-accordion and also as a dancer. She began piano lessons with a Mrs Piper, but taught herself to play the piano-accordion. By the time she was 12 years old she had already appeared in pantomime in Bristol. Olive, who is now in her seventies, has taught dancing in Grangetown for many years. She is well-known for her troupe, the 'Olivettes'! This year will be their 21st year in Cardiff pantomime. Many of Olive's ex-pupils are now teaching, some overseas. Over the years, the children from this dancing school have given many shows at St David's Hospital and are famous for their charity work. Olive was married to the late Steve Gibson.

Many people will remember the houseboats moored along the tide field from the Marl to the Clarence Bridge. There was a short cut through Perkins' Coal Yard in Cambridge Street which led to the houseboats in what is now Avondale Road.

These residents of Madras Street are looking forward to their outing by luxury coach, 1948. The street has since been demolished.

Street parties were held all over the country on 2 June 1953 to celebrate the coronation of Queen Elizabeth II. These residents of Hewell Street joined in the festivities on that day at their own street party.

A party in Llanmaes Street to celebrate the Coronation in 1953.

Alderman George Llewelyn Ferrier JP and Mrs Myfanwy Ferrier pictured during Alderman Ferrier's year of office as Lord Mayor in 1954. The Ferriers kept a grocer's shop on the corner of Cornwall Street and Warwick Street. Later, they ran a wholesale warehouse in North Clive Street.

Grangetown children enjoying a picnic on the Marl in the 1950s. The ground has been levelled and would be unrecognisable to the men who supped ale here before the turn of the century (see page 27).

Hancock's dray-horses, outside the Neville Hotel, on the corner of Clare Road and Cornwall Street, in 1955. The Neville was granted its license on 10 September 1889.

The Plymouth Hotel in Holmesdale Street, licensed in 1847. In October 1882, the Old Brewery, Cardiff, which had already been in operation for well over a century and a half was bought by Samuel Arthur Brain and his uncle, Joseph Benjamin Brain. S.A. Brain became a councillor in 1885 and Mayor of Cardiff in 1899. His record of achievement was impressive: in 1882 beer was supplied to 11 public houses; by 1900 over 80 public houses were owned or leased by the company and output had increased tenfold from 100 to over 1,000 barrels a week.

The Lord Windsor, also in Holmesdale Street, was first licensed in 1893.

The Grange Hotel, situated in Penarth Road, was probably granted its first license in October 1891. In 1903, however, it was recorded as serving any refreshment asked for apart from intoxicants.

The Bird In Hand stood on the corner of Bromsgrove Street and Hewell Street. It was on record as having a license on 3 January 1898 though the date of the original license is not given. The building came down when Hewell Street was demolished.

Mrs Gladys Hall seen here being made an Alderman of the City in the early 1960s. Mrs Hall, who grew up in Eisteddfod Street (where the Empire Pool currently stands) was married at St Paul's Church in 1922 and lived all her married life in Grangetown. She was a life-long member of the Labour Party receiving a certificate for 50 years service from the then leader, Jim Callaghan, on 13 February 1978. After being made an Alderman, Mrs Hall served on various committees and was also involved with the management committee of the Clydach Street day centre. Her husband, Albert Hall, a cabinet maker with David Morgan's for 30 years, was also a councillor.

Joan Gallagher (*née* Hall) pictured (left) is the only child of Mr and Mrs Hall (above). She is seen here in Auxiliary Territorial Service (ATS) uniform when she was stationed in Exeter during the Second World War. Joan followed her parents by also becoming a councillor for Grangetown. She served for four years on the County Council and nine years as a City Councillor.

The expression 'Grangetown boy makes good' is surely true of James Lyons who has been doubly honoured being knighted by both HM The Queen and the Pope (right). This is a rare and notable achievement and the day he received this letter from the palace must have been a very memorable one. There are only about 600 Papal Knights in the whole of the UK. The Knighthood is granted for outstanding duty to the Roman Catholic Church. Nominations go to the parish priest who passes the names on to the archbishop and from there to the Papal Nuncio.

BUCKINGHAM PALACE

12th October, 1979

Sir,

I have the honour to inform you that The Queen has been graciously pleased to grant to you unrestricted permission to wear the insignia of a Knight Commander of the Order of St. Gregory the Great which has been conferred upon you by

His Holiness Pope John Paul II

in recognition of your services.

I have the honour to be, Sir,
Your obedient Servant,

Sir James Lyons.

Sir James Lyons as Lord Mayor giving the Loyal Address outside the City Hall on the occasion of the royal visit in December 1968.

On the occasion of the visit of Pope John Paul II to Cardiff in 1982 Philip Dunleavy of Merches Gardens was Lord Mayor. Mr Dunleavy, a Freeman of the City (since 1993) became a magistrate in 1961 and was Leader of Cardiff City Council (1974-76). He was Labour leader during redevelopment of the city centre and took a personal lead in setting priorities for housing and recreation for every part of the city. He first entered politics when he was refused permission to use school premises for his youth club in Grangetown. Over the years Mr Dunleavy worked tirelessly for the welfare of Cardiff and was passionate about the needs of Grangetown. In 1983, he was awarded the CBE for his service to the city; he died in January 1996. Grangetown has, in fact, given Cardiff seven Lord Mayors the first one being Mr (later Sir) Arthur Ernest Gough in 1933, also of Merches Gardens. On the left of Mr Dunleavy in the picture is the late Mr Ronald J. Watkiss CBE of Pentre Street. Mr Watkiss ran a carpet shop in Clare Road and was Lord Mayor of Cardiff in 1981.

Another Lord Mayor from Grangetown was John Smith (centre) who took office in 1990.

Three
Churches and Chapels

St Paul's parish was formerly a part of the parish of St John's, Canton and in the early days of the community's development there was no church building in Grangetown. A group of people used to meet for divine worship in what was known as Vanstone's Loft over a stable in North Street. When the Baroness Windsor had the National Church School built in 1864, the congregation moved from Vanstone's Loft and Sunday services were held at the National School for many years. In 1879 Lady Mary Windsor Clive gave £500 for an Iron Mission Church – 'The Iron Room'. It was intended to proceed with the permanent structure almost immediately and the utmost economy was therefore exercised in its construction. The deeds for the erection of the permanent building were prepared but the sudden death of the Baroness prevented them from being signed. It was reported in The Cardiff Argus of 17 August 1889, after Lord Windsor laid the foundation stone of the permanent building, that 'It would be, perhaps impossible to find now, in any district with a population of 2,000 or 3,000 persons a more unsightly, inconvenient, and unsuitable iron structure made to serve as a place of divine worship than St Paul's Grangetown: this surprise is increased by a glance round the adjacent streets, where there are numbers of comfortable, convenient and even handsome places of worship erected by the Non conformists.' The consecration of the new St Paul's Church building took place on Wednesday 5 February 1890 at 4 o'clock in the afternoon, and was reported in the parish magazine of St John's, Canton. The Bishop, clergy and choristers marched in procession from the Iron Mission Room arriving at the west door where Lord Windsor met them and presented to the Bishop a request to 'dedicate this House to the worship of Almighty God and the Salvation of Souls'. In 1894 St Paul's was created as a separate parish in its own right and the Revd F.P. Hill was installed by the Bishop of Llandaff as its first vicar in October of that year.

To trace the history of St Patrick's parish it is necessary to go back to the begining of the nineteenth century when the demand for Catholic emancipation began to make itself heard. It is recorded in 1820 that there were three Catholics in Cardiff who occasionally secured the services of a Newport priest to say Mass. Around 1825 Mass was being celebrated in a room of a house in 21 Union Buildings. With the passing of the Catholic Emancipation Act in 1829 the number of Catholics openly-worshipping in Cardiff increased rapidly and a parochial life started to develop with the settlement of Welsh, English, Irish and foreign Catholics. In June 1854 Father Fortunatus Signini of the Fathers of Charity (at the request of the Catholic Bishop of Newport) was sent to take spiritual charge of the 6,000 Catholics in Cardiff. By 1866 he had opened a number of schools in the town, including one at Grangetown which was first used for divine worship in 1869, when Mass was said by Father Stephen Bruno. It was not until 1873, however, that there was any record that this building, which served the needs of about 500 Catholics in Grangetown, was called St Patrick's School.

Grangetown Baptist Church has been in existence for over 130 years. An old minute book of the church bears this entry: 'The English Baptist Church at Lower Grange originated in the self-denying labours of brethren connected with the church at Tredegarville, Roath'. Sunday school and preaching services were held in 1865 and one of the two meeting places was over 'Morley's Stable', on the corner of Earl Street. In 1867 Tredegarville decided, that the Lord's Supper be celebrated in the afternoon of the second Sunday in each month at Grangetown. The first church was opened in 1875 and only six years later the friends at the Grange were united into an independent church and the formation service was held in February 1881. The second church was erected in 1887 at a cost of £1,160 with seating accomodation for 500. The foundation stone which bore the inscription – 'This stone was laid by a working man' – was placed by John Venn who had learnt his trade as a stone mason with E. Turner & Sons. John Venn was the great-grandfather of Bill Dadd, the present owner of Koda Press (see p. 85).

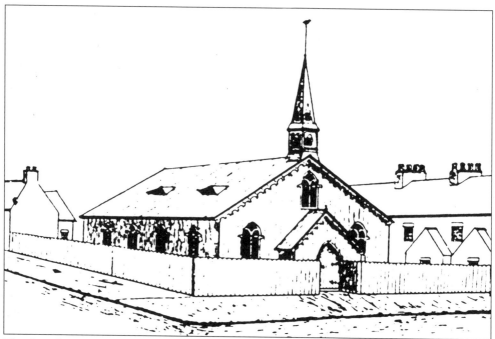

The first Grangetown Baptist Church was the 'iron church' erected in 1875 and opened on 8 December that year. The entire cost of the building was £400. Of this sum, £350 was in hand by the opening day.

With the increase in the number of church members, Mr James Turner submitted a scheme to convert the church into a schoolroom with several classrooms, and to build a new church on the site of the old 'iron church'. Messrs E. Turner & Sons were responsible for the erection of this new building which cost £2,750. Both the Sunday school and church were opened by January 1902.

Grangetown Baptist Church Whitsun treat, 1912.

The pastor and deacons of Grangetown Baptist Church in 1916. Mr W.H. Turner is fourth from the left in the back row.

Mr Harry Turner, son of Mr William Turner, joined the family building firm after returning from the First World War where he was badly wounded outside Jerusalem and was awarded the Military Cross. He gave a lifetime of service to the Baptist cause. He was a life deacon, Sunday school superintendent of Grangetown Baptist Church for over forty years, a member of the Baptist Council of Great Britain and Ireland, chairman of the South Wales Baptist College, and chairman and treasurer of the South Wales Area Joint Board of the Baptist Union.

The Cradle Roll certificate of Edith Shute, dated September 1917. It is signed by W.H. Turner who at that time was superintendent of Clive Street Baptist Sunday school.

The foundation stone of St Patrick's Church was laid by the Archbishop of Cardiff, the Most Revd Francis Mostyn on St Patrick's Day, 1929. The ceremony took place in the presence of about 4,000 men from all the Catholic parishes of Cardiff and a great concourse of people. Exactly one year later, on St Patrick's Day, 1930, the new church was opened.

The Archbishop of Cardiff and supporting members of the clergy at the opening of St Patrick's Church on 17 March 1930.

A letter dated 1869 from Lord Windsor to the church warden during negotiations for the building of St Paul's Church.

The Iron Room. In 1879 Lady Mary Windsor Clive, who took a great interest in Grangetown and was a frequent visitor to the National School, gave £500 for the erection of the Iron Mission Church. The Grange Albion Sports and Social Club now occupies this site.

St Paul's Church. Lord Windsor gave an acre of land on which to build this church in 1885. He built the nave at a cost to himself of £4,000 and personally laid the foundation stone in 1889. The church was consecrated in 1890 by the Bishop of Llandaff, the Rt. Revd R. Lewis DD.

Interior of St Paul's Church.

Whitsun treat at St Paul's in the 1950s showing the Revd C.R. Care and Joyce Cridland (daughter of H.J. Cridland) before they married. The Revd Care was curate at St Paul's from 1944 until 1957. After he and Joyce were married they lived in Penhevad Street.

St Paul's youth club enjoying icecream on a trip to Tenby. The Revd Care is in the centre of the group.

William Jones, who was the founder of Cornwall Street Baptist Chapel. The chapel which was built at Mr Jones' own cost (£1,000) was given to the trustees by his widow. In 1894, a group of worshippers from Bethany Baptist Church, then situated in The Hayes, felt that a church should be established in Grangetown. A church was duly founded by William Jones in Cornwall Road (now Cornwall Street) and opened in 1895.

The interior of Cornwall Street Baptist Chapel as it is today.

Members of the Mothers Union of St Samson's Church, 1930. By order of the Bishop on 31 March 1924, St Samson's district of St Mary's, together with the district of St Paul's parish served by the mission church of St Barnabas were united to form the parish of St Samson.

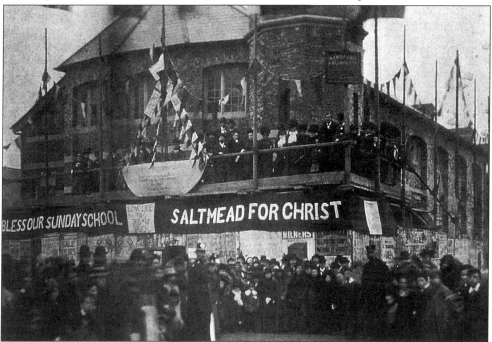

Saltmead Presbyterian Hall. This was opened by the founder of the Welsh Calvinistic Methodist Forward Movement, Dr John Pugh in 1901. Saltmead took a battering in the blitz of the Second World War and the church was badly damaged when landmines dropped nearby. Funds were not available to restore this building which had seating capacity for around 700 people. As the congregation had dwindled, it was decided to sell off the church ground for housing and convert the church hall for worship. A new church was opened in 1993.

Siloam Welsh Baptist Chapel in Corporation Road was opened in 1902. When it closed in the 1950s it was taken over by the Salvation Army, and is now the headquarters of the Grangetown Corps.

A small group of Grangetown Salvationists holding an open-air service in Stafford Road. A feature of the Salvation Army's work in general and in particular the work of the Grangetown Corps over the past 100 years has been the open air meetings, where the band has an important 'mood-setting' role.

Four years after the Salvation Army began its work in Cardiff, a corps was established in Grangetown (1884). It was known then as Cardiff IV (later Cardiff Grangetown) Corps and began with the arrival of Captain Bessie Penwarm. Among the earliest pioneers were John Begg and his family, together with Louise Norton (right), who was to become the first soldier on the roll. She was the grandmother of the present 'No. 1' on the roll, Mrs C. Nurse. The first meetings of the Salvation Army in Grangetown were held in various lofts above stables and stores in Holmesdale Street. The constant 'bombardment' by the fiercely temperance Salvation Army played a great part in the closing down of the Sunday drinking booths on the Marl (see page 27).

Bandmaster Jim Nurse who assumed control of the band in 1932, continuing for many of the next fifty years as leader of the Songster Brigade. In 1955 the Corps was evicted from its hall in Kent Street. The empty Welsh Baptist Chapel in Corporation Road was eventually purchased and the official opening took place in July 1956. Bandmaster Nurse retired in 1978.

BUCKINGHAM PALACE

From: The Assistant Private Secretary to H.R.H. The Prince of Wales

5th September, 1984.

Dear Captain Hughes

The Prince of Wales has asked me to thank you for your recent letter concerning the Centenary Celebrations of the Salvation Army in Cardiff Grangetown.

His Royal Highness and The Princess of Wales were most interested to hear of these celebrations and are grateful to you for taking the trouble to write as you did.

Their Royal Highnesses have asked me to pass on to you and all members of the Cardiff Grangetown Salvation Army their very best wishes for the future.

Yours sincerely

David Roycroft.

Captain Alexandra Hughes.

A letter from Buckingham Palace on the occasion of the Salvation Army's centenary (1884-1994) in Grangetown.

William Edward Davies, or 'Brother Bill' as he was known, was born in a small terraced house at 14 Bromfield Street on 5 August 1914. He grew up to be a great preacher, having attended Ebenezer Gospel Hall with his seven brothers and sisters from early childhood. Most of his life was spent as an itinerant evangelist and Bible teacher in the UK and abroad. His brother, Len Davies, wrote a book about Bill's life and work and called it *Brother Bill*. Vicount Tonypandy wrote in the foreword to the book: 'God has been good to me to let my life be touched by his faithful servant, Bill Davies'.

Ebenezer Gospel Hall Missionary Conference in 1913. 'Ebenezer' had its roots in an old warship HMS *Thisbe* which had seen the end of its service and was moored permanently in Cardiff Docks. The ship was owned by the Church of England and was used as a mission from which vigorous evangelism was carried out for many years. As a result of attending the services aboard the *Thisbe* many mature men were converted and their witness led to many others committing themselves to Christ. These men drew vast crowds when they preached on a Sunday night (out of doors) at Pier Head. A large room above a stable was obtained and called 'Seaman's Bethel'. To provide a substantial building to cater for increasing membership Ebenezer Gospel Hall was built in Corporation Road in 1899 at a total cost of £1,250.

The Forward Movement Grangetown Hall Presbyterian Church. This church stood on the corner of Corporation Road and Paget Street at Penarth Road traffic lights. It was demolished in the 1960s.

Ludlow Street Methodist Church Sunday school children rehearsing for their anniversary in 1956.

Four
Church Schools and State Schools

Formal education, as we know it today, took a while to become fully established in Grangetown as elsewhere in the country. In Cardiff there was a school as early as the reign of Elizabeth I for there is evidence of a school master by the name of John John residing in 'Crockerton'. Then in 1650 a school was set up in Cardiff under the Commonwealth scheme for providing education. Various small schools were also set up through the years run by those with perhaps no greater qualification than the ability to read and write. Occasionally a local curate or preacher would open a small school to supplement his limited income. For example, the Revd Samuel Richards (d.1740), said to be learned in Latin and Greek, successfully conducted a school where older pupils from Cardiff and a wider neighbourhood were taught, including some boarders. In 1777, the Town Council, showing a greater interest in the education of its children, merged the Herbert Trust with the Cradock Wells Trust. By July 1815 a new and public scheme had been drawn up for the establishment of a Charity School for children of all denominations under the presidency of the Marquis of Bute. The school continued to be supported by public subscription and by 1840 it was accomodating about 200 boys and girls. This school eventually became attached to the church for the education of the poor of the parish. Throughout the 1860s there was a sizeable Roman Catholic community in Grangetown. Two priests who came to Cardiff in 1839 pioneered the cause of education with the Irish immigrants. One of these priests, Father Signini, opened a school in Grangetown in 1866 for about 300 pupils. It was a 'ramshackle' affair, however, and totally inadequate for the pressing need for education provision in the area. But it was not until 1871 that the Marquis of Bute, a great benefactor of Catholic schools, offered his generosity to Grangetown. In September of that year Father Signini signed a contract for the building of the school which was eventually erected at a cost of £844 12s 0d in St Patrick's Roman Catholic School in Grangetown.

Grange National Mixed School, or the 'Nash' as it is called by some people, was opened on the 26 January 1864. The Revd Vincent Saulez, Rector of St John's Church, Canton, of which St Paul's was then a mission, gave the inaugural address with the master, Mr G. Ellis, and the 44 children who made up the school, present. By May of that year the number of pupils had risen to 110. The subjects taught were scripture, reading, and arithmetic. That same year the name was changed to St Paul's Church in Wales Primary School. In 1965 the school was visited by a famous 'old boy' – the Rt. Hon. Herbert ('Bertie') Bowden. He was the son of a Grangetown baker and through a successful political career rose to become Leader of the House of Commons and Lord President of the Council (1964-66), eventually being elevated to the peerage as Lord Aylestone. He had been a pupil at the 'Nash' in 1913 at the age of eight. In June 1974 as the school had moved to a modern open-plan building, the old 'Nash' building was demolished.

Grangetown National School. This was the original building and on the extreme left can be seen part of the old police station.

Pupils at Grangetown National School in 1927.

St Patrick's School was opened in March 1873. When the school was built it was practically surrounded by countryside which made it very difficult to reach, especially in winter. Ditches and streams had to be crossed before getting to the school and people in Thomas Street hung their washing on hedges and bushes. Two years after the school was opened many families left the Grange because of the flood (see page 25).

Some of St Patrick's pupils in 1932.

St Patrick's Junior School staff in 1964. From left to right, top row: Miss M. Barry, Mr P.B. Hallett, Miss S.B. Parie, Mr D.J. Davies, Mr D. Cunliffe. Seated: Mr T.N. Spear, Revd Fr Mannion, Mr T. Stevens, Very Revd Canon T.P. Phelan, Mrs J. Steer, Mr W.F. Taylor.

In 1973 St Patrick's School celebrated its centenary. Some pupils of that year are pictured here with headteacher Terry Stevens, Canon C.P. Reidy and form master, Mr Fowler.

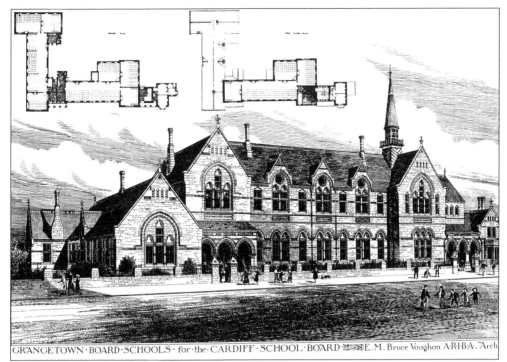

An architect's drawing for the proposed Grangetown Board School taken from *The Building News* of 16 February 1883.

Ninian Park Council School in Virgil Street (originally Virgil Street Board School) which was opened on 30 November 1900. It was renamed Ninian Park Council School in October 1911.

Two photographs taken at the same school but forty years apart. Above, pupils with their teachers at the Virgil Street Board School before the turn of the century and, below, children celebrating St David's Day at Ninian Park Primary School in 1938.

These boys from Grangetown Council School were Cardiff champions in the 1920-21 season. Grangetown Council School, or Grangetown Academy as it was often humorously called, was built well over a hundred years ago. During its construction, after strong winds and heavy rain for some weeks, the high tide swept up the River Taff and flooded parts of Grangetown to a depth of 4 ft. Many residents had to be rescued from their homes by boats. After the waters had receded some people built their own boats in preparation for the next flood which fortunately never came. The teachers were tough at Grangetown Council school. They had to be. One of the teachers was Mr Cornish who was a strict disciplinarian. He and another teacher Charlie Buck frequently gave six of the best with their bamboo cane to disobedient lads.

The staff of Grangetown Council school, in 1948.

These two photographs show pupils at Court Road School. Above, at the Girls School in 1939 and, below, at the Infants School in 1948. Court Road School suffered in the blitz along with Saltmead church and was demolished with the reorganisation of schools into a comprehensive system.

Five

Business and
Industrial Ventures

It is impossible to recount the history of Grangetown without including the famous family name of Turner, or, in fact, to tell the story of Cardiff without lengthy praise for the work of E. Turner & Sons of Grangetown. Without the Turner family Cardiff would not exist as we see it today as they built not only the Civic Centre buildings well known throughout Europe and the world but also most of the buildings in the central shopping area, and many churches – St Patrick's Church and the Baptist Church in Grangetown to name just two.

Ephraim Turner was born in the late 1830s in Merthyr. His father had been attracted by the potential wealth to be gained there during the industrial revolution and had left his farm in Herefordshire to seek his fortune in Wales. Ephraim grew up in Merthyr, became a builder and married in 1860. His son, James Edward, was born the following year and William Henry Turner was born in 1866. By the time the family moved to Grangetown in 1870, Ephraim had earned a reputation as a builder of some of the fine old stone-arch bridges on the LMS (London, Midland and Scottish Railway) line into Merthyr. In 1885 the business of E. Turner & Sons was founded by Ephraim in Cardiff with his two sons. The business went from strength to strength and by the time Queen Victoria celebrated her Diamond Jubilee in June 1897 both Ephraim's sons were in complete control. On that day when reminders of royalty were everywhere, Ephraim may well have thought of the day in the previous year when the Prince of Wales (the future Edward VII) came to Cardiff to wonder with others at the splendour of the latest fine Turner building, when he opened the new library extension in The Hayes. Also, in 1896, Turner's built the General Post Office on the corner of Westgate Street.

In the last decade of the nineteenth century Turner's were building over a thousand houses to absorb the seven thousand extra inhabitants each year. Between 1890 and 1897 they built forty-seven churches and chapels as well as almost five hundred shops and twenty schools. They employed five hundred men and the wage bill was £25,000 a year – an average of £1 a week per employee. In those days a fine house cost around £400. Cardiff, at the turn of the century, was the boom town of South Wales. It had been growing rapidly under the impetus of 'coal fever' and had become the greatest coal-exporting part in the world. Turner's at this time secured the contract for the building of the new Town Hall and the Law Courts. This contract worth £200,000 was carried out under the personal supervision of both James and William Turner and was completed in 1904.

These were busy days and while steam had come to sea and rail, the horse was still used by road. The stone for the new Civic Centre was brought by ship from Portland. The company had forty shire horses for transporting the stone from the docks. It must have been a spectacular sight to watch the six teams of shires pulling the twelve to fifteen ton blocks of stone from the docks to the stone yard in Grangetown.

Left: Mr Ephraim Turner. Right: Mr James Turner.

The offices of E. Turner & Sons stood in Havelock Place with a blacksmith's shop and a yard at the back of the premises. The building was demolished a few years ago after fire damage and a block of new houses and flats now occupies the site.

Turner's joiner's shop was spacious, airy, well-heated, well-lit and thoroughly equipped. Special attention was paid to the all important 'glueing' and there was a separate area with a heating system which enabled a suitable temperature for 'glueing' to be maintained in all weathers.

These stonemasons were just a few of the hundreds of skilled men employed by Turner's over the years. By their hands were shaped Cardiff's magnificent Civic Centre and many buildings in England and Wales. Swansea's Guildhall and the beautiful restoration of St Mary's Church are two other examples of their work.

An artist's impression of 'Min-yr-Avon' or 'Turner's Mansion' as it was called when it was first built by William Turner. He lived here until his death. The house is now called 'The Inn on the River' and has been a pub for about twenty years.

A family portrait taken in 1910 to celebrate the golden wedding anniversary of Ephraim Turner and his wife, Ann. The house 'Cefn Coed', which they built in the 1890s, has been demolished.

Another well-known builder in Grangetown was Eugene Addicott, who built the Ely housing estate. He became a member of the Union of Building Trade Workers in 1899. The Addicott family lived in Saltmead Road (now Stafford Road) then moved to Corporation Road.

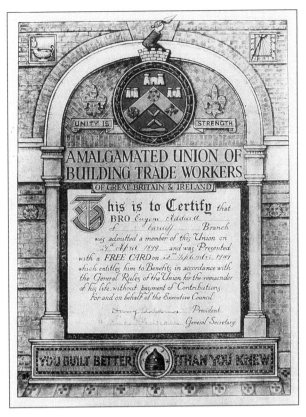

Some of the men who were employed by Eugene Addicott in 1937.

Hancock's Brewery in Crawshay Street before (above), and after (below) fire gutted the building in 1911.

Another business to suffer a serious fire was the White Heather Laundry in Mardy Street which was completely gutted in 1908.

'Kosirest' – White Wilson's furniture and bedding factory. It was situated on the site of the old horse-drawn tram depot in York Place, where the 'asthmatic' old gas engines chugged away day and night. The engines have long since gone but happily the factory still survives.

One of the many Co-op stores, which sprang up in the early years of the century, was situated in Clare Road. The Co-operative Wholesale Society was established in Manchester in 1864 as a development from the early co-operative experiments of Robert Owen and the 'Rochdale Pioneers'. Consumers were encouraged to form their own retail societies and share the profits among themselves thus eliminating the middle man.

R.B. Flowers originally had a shop in Wood Street and when the streets around that area were demolished the firm moved to Grangetown. This was their shop on the corner of Sussex Street and Cornwall Street in 1915.

Bill Batstone had a greengrocery and fishmonger round. He is pictured here in Universal Street in 1927.

One of the corner-shops in 1927 was Moorcraft's grocery on the corner of Hewell Street and Worcester Street.

J.R Freeman & Son Ltd, cigar manufacturers, opened a factory in Cardiff in 1908 and were operating in North Clive Street by 1911. This photograph of their employees was taken in 1926. The factory continued to expand and by 1961 was operating from premises in Penarth Road. The factory currently employs around 400 workers.

Some of the staff employed by the rope works in Gasworks Road, 1929. Among them is amateur Welsh boxing champion Jack Pottinger, second from the left in the front row.

H.J. Cridland, second left, with his sons William, Albert and Tommy, 1919. This well-known family business in Grangetown was started by Henry John Cridland (known locally as 'H.J.'). At 13 years of age he started working for an Italian wine importer on the docks. His job was to bottle the wine; often, however, often he was given 1d to travel on the tram to the town centre on an errand but would run all the way there and back therefore making a penny for himself. Being ambitious and thrifty while working for the Italian, 'H.J.' saved and bought himself a horse and cart. He opened a business opposite his boss and employed someone to work for him at the docks collecting and delivering goods. He married Elizabeth Mitchell and they had six children: four boys and two girls. The eldest girl married Charles Vincent who was an undertaker in Corporation Road in the 1940s. The Cridland business expanded as the family grew up. Sons, Billy, Tommy, and Albert worked in the garage situated at the back of 18 Paget Street. Daughter, Doris, worked in the office with Mr Fred Fabian the clerk. The business had started off with trolleys and cart horses taking goods to the ships on the dock. Then from about 1918, charabancs were used to run outings. Then Cridlands went into the undertaking business, with carriages drawn by black Belgian horses. The horses were eventually replaced at funerals by a Rolls-Royce hearse and three Rolls-Royce saloon cars and lorries were employed in place of the cart horses and carts.

Mr Dick Perry with the hearse. Mr Perry was employed to look after the horses. Coffins were made by a Mr Tom Phillips in an upstairs room at the back of the garage. The walls were covered with planks of wood – oak and elm – for customers to choose the type and quality of coffin required.

Mr Tommy Cridland looking resplendant with coach and pair of black Belgian horses.

Cridland's charabancs. These were used from about 1918 onwards mainly for outings. By 1933 coaches like the one seen below had taken their place. These coaches were used for private hire work until the business closed in the mid-1950s.

One of the fleet of thirteen coaches, which Cridland's bought from S.J. Wood of Blackpool in the 1930s. Some of these Leyland Tiger all-weather coaches had canvas roofs which could be removed.

W. Frank Ltd's sweet factory in Pendyris Street, 1931. The business was started in 1867 and by 1910 Frank's had shops and stalls all over Cardiff.

A 'Vulcan' lorry owned by James Perkins, photographed in Ludlow Close in 1934. The lorry was originally owned by British Petroleum (BP) Ltd.

Mr William ('Bill') Dadd setting type. Koda Press still employs the traditional hot-metal method. The premises in North Clive Street was once occupied by Cridland's undertaking business of which there is still some evidence. In 1990, S4C used Koda Press as the set for their documentary on the life of Silvia Pankhurst.

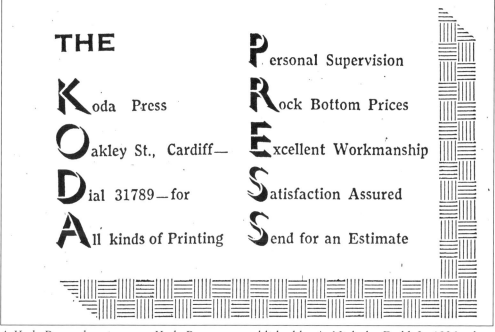

THE

Koda Press

Oakley St., Cardiff—

Dial 31789—for

All kinds of Printing

Personal Supervision

Rock Bottom Prices

Excellent Workmanship

Satisfaction Assured

Send for an Estimate

A Koda Press advertisement. Koda Press was established by A. Nicholas Dadd. In 1926, when the Miners' Strike and economic depression began to take their toll on his livelihood in Tonypandy, he came to Grangetown and opened up the business at 57 Oakley Street. His wife Beatrice, meanwhile, ran the Conibear Drug Store at 61 Oakley Street, with her brother John Conibear. Their eldest son Alfred left school at 14 to join two other apprentices at the family printing firm. When A.N. Dadd died in 1959 the firm was taken over by Alfred. In 1965 Alfred's son Bill took over the business. Koda Press is now situated in North Clive Street, where it was relocated when redevelopment forced a move from Oakley Street.

Mr Alfred V. Dadd (father of the present owner) and Mike Imperato drying the ink on a four-colour magazine.

A family affair. Eva and Alf Dadd and their son Bill take a well-earned coffee break.

Anthony Mahoney, the Clive Street cobbler, was born in Penarth Road and educated at St Patrick's School. He left school at fourteen to become an apprentice shoemaker. After spending six years in the Army he worked at two premises in Penarth Road before renting the shop at Clive Street. He has worked there for the past thirty-five years, initially with George Thompson who retired in 1974.

These advertisements show some of the businesses which have been well-known in Grangetown over the years. Note the four-figure phone numbers.

Painters employed at Grangetown gasworks, 1912.

The original control room at the Grangetown plant.

A fleet of 'Sentinel' steam-lorries at Grangetown gasworks in 1928. In 1836, a meeting was held at the Cardiff Town Hall under the chairmanship of the Mayor and it was resolved that a company should be formed to be called 'The Cardiff Gas and Coke Company, for effectually lighting the town, the present gasworks being wholly insufficient for the purpose.' As a result of this meeting a special Act of Parliament was passed – 'An Act for better lighting with gas of the town of Cardiff in the county of Glamorgan'. This was given Royal Assent in 1837. It became necessary to enlarge the gasworks in 1847 and again in 1851. In 1854, gas supplies were extended to Canton. A further extension of the works became necessary and a new gasholder having a capacity of 200,000 cubic feet was built. The new Act of 1854 gave the company, powers to supply gas to the outlying parishes of Llandaff, Leckwith, Llandough, Penarth, and Roath. The additional demands would put a great strain on the already congested works of Bute Terrace and it became necessary to consider a larger site and new works. Land was found and acquired in Grangetown in 1859 and a new works was built and brought into operation in 1865. Gas production continued at Bute Terrace until 1907 when the old works was shut down and manufacture was centralised at Grangetown.

Aerial view of the gasworks, c. 1950. Coke and tar were produced as by-products in considerable quantities and were in great demand.

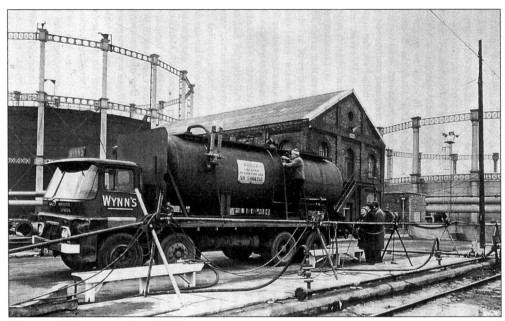

Home-made butane tanker, 1963.

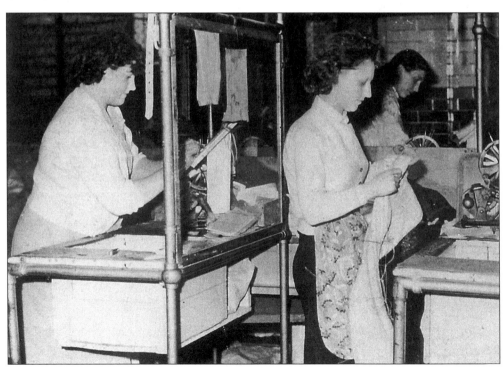

Women workers at the New Era Laundry in Pendyris Street, 1959.

Six

Two World Wars

'The maxim of the British people' in Winston Churchill's words in November 1914 was 'business as usual' and serious efforts were made to maintain the normal pattern of public and private life during the First World War (1914-1918). Inevitably, however, the hostilities soon began to affect everyone and everything. Thousands of men either volunteered for or were called up to the armed forces and a Cardiff City Battalion of the Welsh Regiment was formed. Many contracts for new buildings – as with The National Museum of Wales – had to be cancelled because of the increasing shortage of materials, the considerable limitations on transport and the increasing prices. The entire fleet of the Cardiff company, Neale & West, was commandeered for mine-sweeping. Many men and women were thrown into manufacturing work new to them. Teaching courses were therefore established in Cardiff and elsewhere and the building of the Technical College in Cathays Park was pressed forward and finished in 1916.

From 1915 onwards the impact began to take visible form. 'Public lighting was drastically reduced; schools and hospitals were requisitioned for military purposes; arrangements for the protection of important public buildings and undertakings were put in hand.' Even the opening hours of public houses were cut under the Defence of the Realm Act of March 1915.

The War Savings Movement was launched and works were undertaken by the City Council to relieve unemployment caused by the dislocation of trade and industry; women began to replace men in jobs hitherto regarded as male preserves – for example, as drivers and conductors on public transport services.

As the food situation worsened, following the enemy's submarine campaign, the government introduced a national system of food control and, in a precursor of the Second World War, rationing was introduced in 1918 and public parks were used as allotments in order to increase food production.

The Second World War (1939-1945) has often been described as a 'The People's War'. No previous conflict in history has so directly involved the civilian populations of the combatant countries. Even before war was formally declared in September 1939, conscription had been introduced in Germany (1934) and Great Britain (earlier in 1939). Once the war began, those who were not called up into the armed forces found themselves to various degrees directed into home defence (the Local Defence Volunteers, later the Home Guard) or into essential work in industry and the mines and vital services such as transport. With the increased capacity of aircraft to bomb distant targets, the civilian's life was also far more at risk than in any previous war, with Cardiff being one of the British cities to be blitzed by the Luftwaffe. Almost all necessities were soon rationed or hard to find even on the 'black market'. To find consumer goods of most kinds – from prams to furniture – necessitated a long search and as coal was directed to the war effort, people often struggled to keep warm in their homes. Food rationing, perhaps, made the deepest impact on most people but, due to the fairer sharing out of supplies, poorer families ate better than they had before the war; rigid price controls kept inflation within limits and by 1945 the cost of living was only a third higher than before the start of the war. Although the years of the Second World War brought hardship to many civilians, as well as the tragedy of lives lost on foreign fronts, they also brought benefits. Far greater government direction of the economy banished the spectre of mass employment from South Wales and it did not return for two generations; women, in particular, gained greater freedom and independence as traditional roles were broken down to meet the demands of the war effort.

Open your door to passers-by — They need shelter too

Tom Purvis, whose wartime poster is shown above, attended Grange Council school in Holmesdale Street around the time of the First World War. His Second World War posters are famous and have now become collector's items.

During the First World War White Wilson's mattress factory was converted into an aviation works. Pictured here are workers in the plane and rib department. The factory was situated at the north end of Penarth Road and Ely Harbour Road (later Ferry Road).

Freeman's Cigar Factory first produced their famous Manikin cigars in Grangetown in 1912. The factory kept producing these cigars throughout the First World War. This photograph shows the girls who were employed at Freeman's at that time.

During the First World War Ninian Park school was converted into a hospital to cope with the large numbers of wounded soldiers returning from the front line.

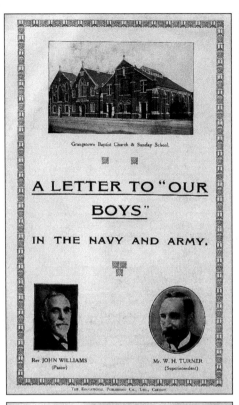

Grangetown Baptist Church & Sunday School.

A LETTER TO "OUR BOYS"

IN THE NAVY AND ARMY.

Rev. JOHN WILLIAMS
(Pastor)

Mr. W. H. TURNER
(Superintendent)

THE EDUCATIONAL PUBLISHING CO., LTD., CARDIFF.

"Ring out, O! happy joy-bells, ring!
While we our glad thanksgiving bring.
The winter-time of war is past,
And flowers of peace appear at last."

We are now cherishing the hope that before long we shall be privileged to extend to you our joyous welcome home.

We cannot help asking ourselves the question "What is going to be the fruit of this great victory?" Is it going to be the punishment of the guilty instigators of this criminal war, however exalted their station and powerful their authority, and the demand for reparation, restitution and indemnity for the wrongs done to persons and property? Yes, all that. But the burning of the thorns and briars of militarism is a small matter compared with the harvesting of the fruit of diligent toil and honest labour of peaceful industry. We can leave that to the politicians. We have paid dearly in blood and treasure for the clearing away of the rubbish of militarism. We must now see that the Temple of Freedom is built upon the solid rock of redeemed manhood, and that the nations are established upon righteousness. Our national leaders must be more than mere politicians, they must be God's servants cherishing high ideals and be determined by the help of God to reduce those ideals into practical deeds of experience. And it is up to us to do our part with them. We owe it to ourselves, we owe it to our children, we owe it to our religious faith, and we owe it to our God and Saviour Jesus Christ, to do all that lies within our power.

In order to do our best, we must put ourselves right with God. That is the starting point. Without Him, we can do nothing. A burnished engine without steam (or its equivalent) is a mere ornament and useless, and we are of little use until the Spirit of God is within us, as the power of God unto salvation both to ourselves and our fellows. That is the safest and happiest condition in which we can live in this world.

We are naturally thinking how we can best serve each other when you are at home again. We are glad to read in your letters what pleasure you derive from the remembrance of the happy time you used to spend with us in Church and Sunday School. We want that pleasure increased on your return home. We want to form a League of Comradeship for our mutual benefit, both temporal and spiritual; and any suggestions you may wish to make in regard to that we shall be pleased to consider them. Our time here is short, and we want to make the best use of it. Since we issued the last list of our "Boys" a few changes have taken place as indicated in the subjoined list. We feel sure you would desire to join us in expression of sincere sympathy with the bereaved families.

To Our "Boys" in the Navy and Army

Dear Comrades,

It is with a gladsome mind and a joyful heart that we send you our Christmas Greetings this time, and never before have we with warmer affection expressed the old time greeting of "A Merry Christmas and a Happy New Year to you all." Whilst we at home were cherishing the hope that the fighting would be over by Christmas, none of us dared to be so certain as some of you seemed to be according to your letters sent home. Now that the fighting is over our joy is mutual and our gratitude is up-lifting.

Our first impulse in writing was to ask you to join us in singing the Doxology on the signing of the "Armistice" on November 11th, 1918, but on second thoughts, we were fully persuaded that you had already done it over and over again, as we here had done, and who could refrain from doing it? We were all hilarious in our joy! "Armistice Day" is written on our memory as it was written on many a letter and post-card sent home from the "Front," and it will remain a day never to be forgotten.

Our second impulse was to shout our deepest gratitude into the air so that the breezes of heaven, like wireless telegraphy, might waft it on to you, you, our brave and gallant boys, who on sea and land had so nobly played your part in gaining such a signal victory over an unscrupulous enemy. We know what you will say to that, yea, *you* who have endured and suffered most (except those who have fallen), "We only did our duty!" But that is saying much, and our warmest gratitude is a poor reward for your heroic endurance of the hardships of war. Thank God, all that is nearly over now, and the feeling of relief that has come to us and you is indescribable. There is more music in our speech, softness in our voice, and elasticity in our step so that we go about our work with a lighter heart and a brighter spirit. We have been delivered from what the Psalmist would have described as "the pains of hell" that had got hold of us. Verily "the Lord has done great things for us, whereof we are glad." "His right hand and His holy arm has gotten us the victory."

It was a great joy to us all to welcome home our comrade, Edwin Taylor, who was a prisoner of war in Germany. We were glad to see him looking comparatively well.

By the time this is printed, two of our "Boys" will have been baptized, thus becoming "Soldiers of the King." We pray that many more will follow their example.

We ask your kind acceptance of the enclosed P.O., as an expression (though a very inadequate one) of our love and esteem. On Christmas morning we shall again be meeting for prayer, seeking on your behalf, the protection and guidance of our Heavenly Father. Commending you to His loving care, and with the heartiest "good wishes for the Season" from all in Church and Sunday School,

We are,

Yours in the highest service,

JOHN WILLIAMS (Pastor),
(74, Taff Embankment, Cardiff).

W. H. TURNER (Superintendent),
(Min-yr-Avon, Taff Embankment, Cardiff).

IN LOVING MEMORY OF

L.Cpl. Archie Barrow, Killed in France.

Pte. Alfred J. Horsey, Killed in France.

Leading-Seaman George R. Rees, Killed by enemy's action.

To Our " Boys " in the Navy and Army

Dear Comrades,

It is with a gladsome mind and a joyful heart that we send you our Christmas Greetings this time, and never before have we with warmer affection expressed the old time greeting of " A Merry Christmas and a Happy New Year to you all." Whilst we at home were cherishing the hope that the fighting would be over by Christmas, none of us dared to be so certain as some of you seemed to be according to your letters sent home. Now that the fighting is over our joy is mutual and our gratitude is up-lifting.

This is an enlargement of the first paragraph from the letter opposite, sent by the Revd John Williams (Pastor) and W.H. Turner (Superintendent) on behalf of Grangetown Baptist Church and Sunday School to 'Our Boys' in the Army and Navy.

The plaque in Cornwall Street Baptist Chapel commemorates those brave men who gave their lives in the First World War (1914-1918).

The memorial in Grange Gardens to the Grangetown heroes who fell in the First World War. This was erected entirely from voluntary subscriptions collected by the War Heroes memorial committee with Mr W.H. Turner as president of the fund. Grangetown boys are recorded here as having lost their lives serving with the Royal Welch Fusiliers, South Wales Borderers, 2nd and 3rd Welch Regiments, The Royal Army Medical Corps, Royal Engineers, Royal Field Artillery, Machine Gun Corps, Royal Navy and Merchant Navy.

The inscription on the base of the memorial bears the name W.H. Turner so we can safely assume that this monument was the product of Turner's stonemasons.

In the years preceding the Second World War many 'unemployment clubs' were formed to help ease the situation of the mass unemployment of the 1920s and 1930s, a catastrophe which eased as the thirties progressed and which was soon to be rectified with the outbreak of the Second World War in 1939 and the consequent mass demand for recruits for the forces and labour for the war economy. The lads, above, were on holiday for a week in 1939.

Grangetown was badly hit by the blitz on 2 January 1941. This was how the house on the corner of Ferry Road and Holmesdale Street looked the morning after the raid.

Another casualty of the blitz in January 1941 was the Supolstery works in Ferry Road. It was one of the many buildings destroyed that night, when more than a hundred German bombers raided the city.

Scenes like this were typical all over the country after the air-raids with people salvaging what they could from their bombed-out dwellings. At this house in Grangetown people were rescuing as many of their belongings as possible.

These two views of Jubilee Street show the extent of the destruction that took place. There was no doubt that the Saltmead area along with Riverside suffered the worst damage. Most of the parachute mines landed in this area and caused much destruction.

From June 1940 to May 1943 Cardiff endured a number of air-raids. The residential areas of Riverside and Saltmead suffered the brunt of these attacks but the night of 2 January 1941 was the worst. Early on in the raid (which began at 6.37 p.m. on a freezing night) a shelter at Hollyman's Bakery, at the junction of Corporation Road and Stockland Street, received a direct hit and thirty-two people, including the Hollyman family, were killed outright.

'Dig for victory' was an early wartime slogan coined to promote increased production of food on the home front.

Eileen Cox (now Breslin), 'digging for victory' on the allotments at the back of Clive Street during the Second World War.

Edith Shute, who joined the Women's Voluntary Service (WVS) ambulance service as a driver during the Second World War and served throughout. Her attendant on the ambulance was Miss Nancy Gibbon. At the begining of the war they were stationed at Sloper Road. Edith's day job was at British Ropes but she still worked a twelve-hour night shift on a Wednesday and from three to seven on Sunday nights. Everyone had to take a test before being allowed to drive an ambulance but because of the petrol shortage they were only allowed two practice runs. The ambulance went out after the raids and Edith mostly remembers having to recover bodies to take to the morgue.

Seen arriving home from a prisoner of war camp in the Far East is Corporal Graham Price of Grangetown in 1945.

At last the war was over and the whole country celebrated with street parties. These were the residents of Dorset Street celebrating VE Day in May 1945. Below, the residents of Monmouth Street celebrated with a fancy dress parade.

The VE Day celebrations in Redlaver Street with a party for the children (above) and below for the grown-ups.

This happy crowd in party mood are residents of Compton Street. They were celebrating VJ Day in August 1945.

VJ Day celebrations in Kent Street, August 1945. The 'Dixielanders' played for dancing in the streets and they also helped numerous charities.

Seven
Sport and
Leisure Activities

Grangetown people have always been keen sports enthusiasts. Baseball in Grange can be traced back as far as 1898 and the Grangetown Club. Ten years later this became the Grange Albion Baseball Club. They played on the famous Marl and had their headquarters in the Grange Temperance Institute in Earl Street. In 1908 the first baseball international took place on the turf of Cardiff Arms Park. During most of the exciting and successful years the secretary of the Albion was David Minchington and the treasurer was Bill Smith (a most respected member of the Welsh Baseball Council) while Jimmy Courteny was a notable player. Other players who were of international standard and who did so much to build and maintain the tremendous reputation gained include Vic Lewis, 'Buzzer' Evans, Freddie Fish, Dai Griffiths, Grantley Smith, and Arthur Cornish (whose nephew and namesake was the legendary Cardiff and Wales rugby union player. The Cornishes were a well-known Grangetown family. Arthur lived there, taught in the local school, became headmaster and took part in all the varied sporting activities. Don was a fine soccer full-back, and Doug, another good player, gained promotion in the City Police Force). The baseball club was an important part of the community and was always enthusiastically followed wherever they played. The Albion progressed so well that by the time the Second World War started in 1939 they could boast that they had been Welsh League champions 22 times, had won the Welsh Baseball Challenge Cup 17 times and had produced 21 internationals. The war brought a temporary cessation of baseball activity, but they were off again as soon as it was possible.

Nearby, was the Stockland Rovers Soccer Club which was taken over from the Albion. One of the officials of this club was Jim Brimmell senior, whose son became the well-known boxing referee. Keen on promoting football and stimulating interest the progressive officials sponsored the first inter-city matches. Grange Albion represented Cardiff and played eight 'Wales v England internationals'. The Cardiff XI won six of them!

It was the dream of many of the Albion officials, local councillors, and representatives of other clubs to get all the sports organisations in Grangetown to form one club. It was 1968 before the opportunity presented itself. The 'Grangetown Sports and Social Club' was born and a new era was initiated. It was decided to purchase the ground on which the old 'Iron Room' of St Paul's stood in Paget Street. Raising the money was quite a task but this dedicated group of sportsmen never gave up hope and the building which now stands on the corner of Paget Street is a fitting tribute to their determination. The Sports and Social Club was opened by the then Vicar of St Paul's, the Revd Rendall Jones.

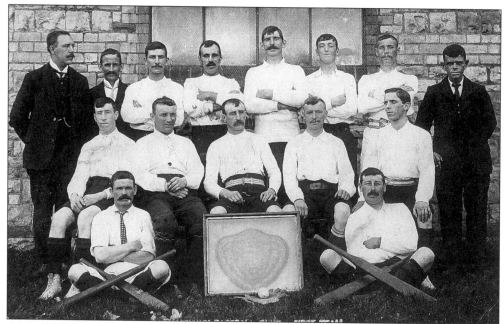

Grangetown's Baseball Club's first-team in 1906.

GRANGE LIBERAL INSTITUTE, A.F.C. Season 1910-11.
Third Row—Mr. E. D. Bumble (Com.) Mr. J. Redman (Com.) Mr. L. Epps (Com.) W. Pearce, C. Morgan, J. Cope (Sec.)
W. Watkins, A. M. Webber, O. Drennan, J. Pearce, R. Carnell (Com.), E. Charlcombe (Com.) W. Sharman.
W. Hoskins, Geo. Hancock.
Second Row—A. Chills, J. Griffiths, A. Brown (Capt.) Geo. Bravey (Vice-Capt.) D. Roberts.
First Row—A. T. Webber, G. Plater, Jim Fearby, Max Gotz.

Grange Liberal Institute AFC in their 1910-11 season.

The opening of the bowling-green in Grange Gardens on 12 June 1906. Built at a cost of £20, the Grange Club was once one of the most successful teams in South Wales. In June 1906 Pettigrew's volume on the 'Public Parks and Recreation Grounds of Cardiff' describes the colourful opening ceremony: 'There was a large gathering of aldermen and councillors and many ladies were in attendance. The green is 40 yards square and is admirable for smoothness. Councillor J.J. Dixon, as deputy chairman of the parks and open spaces committee, declared the green open and was presented with a special pair of bowls. In his opening speech he spoke of the pleasure it would give to see the ancient game alienating their young men from the public houses. It afforded the crowd equal pleasure to witness the zest with which the aldermen and veteran councillors discharged the bowls toward the jack and disported themselves generally. The spectacle was an exhilarating one, a revival of the pleasures of the rustic green, enlivened by the bright costumes of the ladies. In a few months time a little sunshine might rekindle the old spirit and tea will be sipped in the pavilion built by the council to ensure the lost age slips no further away'.

A match in progress on the bowling-green in Grange Gardens shortly after it was opened.

Ladies from Grangetown Gasworks baseball team, pictured after their match in 1918.

Grange Albion baseball team were the undefeated league champions and were winners of the Dewar Shield from 1946 to 1949, and the Welsh Baseball Union Cup 1948-49.

Grangetown Baseball Club in 1908 when they won the Dewar Shield and every one of their 18 matches.

Grangetown RFC, 1908-09 season. Many of the baseball players were rugby and soccer players in the winter months. The rugby lads were mainly from the old St Barnabas RFC or Grange Baptists, one of the really fine Cardiff and District XVs which later became Cardiff (Grange) RFC.

Cardiff and Wales' famous rugby player and teacher, Arthur Cornish, is pictured here on the right with Grange Council baseball team, 1923.

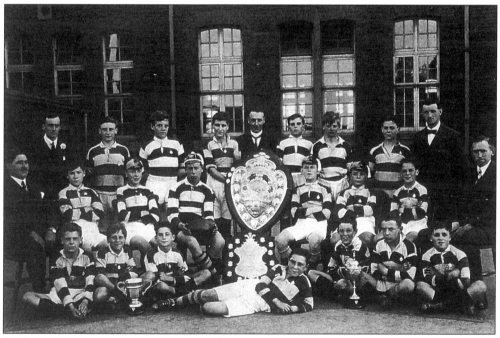

In the 1924-25 season Ninian Park School rugby team won the *South Wales Daily News and Echo* Shield. Their league and cup record was played 29, won 29, points for – 593, points against – 38.

Grange Baptists RFC won numerous cups in the 1920s. Pictured here is the team that represented them in the first round of the Welsh Charity Cup.

Grange Sports Club rugby team in the 1933-34 season.

Well-known amateur flyweight boxer Jack Pottinger won the Welsh Championship between 1934 and 1936. In July 1935 he was one of fourteen young boxers chosen to represent Great Britain against the USA at the Yankee Stadium in New York in a 'Golden Gloves' tournament. The British boys won eight of the contests and triumphantly returned to Britain to be wined and dined at the Grosvenor House Hotel in London.

Grange YMCA Wrestling Club pictured in 1931. They won the Welsh Championship in 1929-30.

Pictured here in the 1920s is Fay Taylor, an accomplished rider in the male-dominated speedway racing world. At her side is Jack 'Lightning' Luke.

In the 1920s and 1930s Grangetown people flocked to the stadium in Sloper Road to enjoy the thrills and spills of these speedway stars. Jack 'Lightning' Luke is second right of the picture. Second left is F.C. 'Hurricane' Hampson.

Known as the Welsh White City Stadium, the Sloper Road speedway and greyhound track is pictured here in 1930, two years after its opening. It was taken over by GKN for their sports ground before being closed in 1981. The site is now occupied by the City Gardens housing development.

Stan 'Broncho' Longney, another of the speedway stars of the 1930s. In those days a grandstand seat cost two shillings and four pence.

St Samson's ladies hockey team, 1930-31.

Grange Wanderers FC, Cup winners in the 1934-35 season.

Many boys from Grange Council School went on to play for the Grange Albion baseball team. Sports master Ivor Beynon's connections with the Welsh Baseball Association made him the ideal talent scout. Ivor is on the left of the group after the school team won the Elliot Seager Shield again in 1934.

Ninian Park School baseball team also won the Elliot Seager Championship Shield many years later in 1948.

Leslie Maidment (extreme right of picture) helped to bring speedway back to Grangetown in 1951, though, unfortunately, not for long. With him are Arthur Pilgrim, Mick Holland, Alf Elliot, Jimmy Wright, Kevin Hayden, and Mick Callaghan. The team looked smart in their green and white jerseys with red dragon. A Dorset man, Leslie Maidment had overheard a Cardiff visitor to his local speedway track at Southhampton bemoaning the fact that speedway racing no longer took place in Cardiff. The following day Leslie travelled to Cardiff with the intention of rectifying the situation. At about the same time in Cardiff, Major A.J. Lennox was thinking along similar lines. Major Lennox, who commanded the 5th Battalion of the Glamorgan Army Cadet Force at the time, was also an accomplished motor-cyclist who had won an impressive array of trophies. He was a member of the London Auto Cycle Union, and had been chairman of the South Wales Auto Cycle Union for the previous 21 years. After several sites for a speedway track were rejected a suitable one was found on land ajacent to the Clarence Bridge. First of all the allotment holders on this land had to be bought out and with the help of a bulldozer the cleaning and levelling of the site took six weeks. Finally the track was completed and opened in October 1950. Speedway racing thus returned to Cardiff after a lapse of around twenty years. Leslie Maidment had contacted Alf Elliot, an old friend who was an expert rider and authority on track construction who once the 400 yard track was open developed a Speedway School to encourage and coach youngsters. In his capacity as team manager of the Dragons he put hundreds of promising lads through their paces.

The Grange Albion Sport and Social Club built on the site of the old 'Iron Room'. When the social club was first opened it was described as 'as sumptuous as one can find', with a main mixed bar, men-only Sportsman's bar and skittle alley.

Grange Albions AFC, 1946-47. That season they were the undefeated league winners, winners of the Lord Ninian Stuart Cup and semi-finalists in the South Wales and Monmouthshire Amateur Cup.

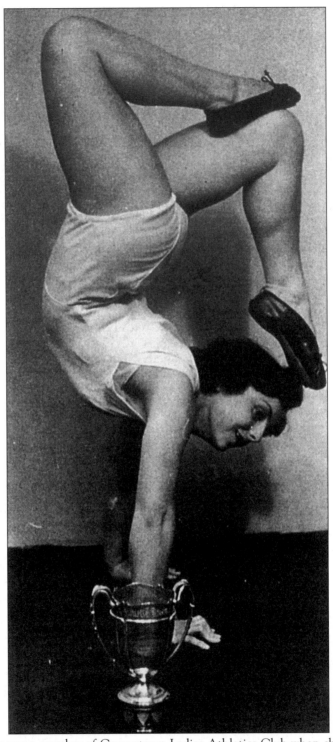

Gwyneth Lewis was a member of Grangetown Ladies Athletics Club when she first won the Welsh Senior Champions trophy in 1951. She represented Great Britain in the 1952 and 1960 Olympic Games and won the individual British gymnastics title in 1959.

Grangetown Ladies Athletic Club. This was their gymnastic display team photographed at the Marl in 1950. Seated, second left in the front row, is Councillor R.G. Shute, father of Edith Shute (see p. 103).

Grange Albion FC during the 1949-50 season.

Mr Sidney Gilmore, secretary of the Grangetown Bowling Club and chairman, Mr L. Madley working by gaslight at the clubhouse in 1962.

The famous boxer David ('Darkie') Hughes won the British lightweight title in 1960. He was a Welsh and British army cadet champion at fifteen and was only beaten in ten out of two hundred and fifty contests. Between 1947 and 1953 he represented Wales with great success becoming Welsh and British ABA light welter-weight champion in 1953. After this he turned professional but gave up his boxing career when he lost the British title to Dave Charnley in 1961.

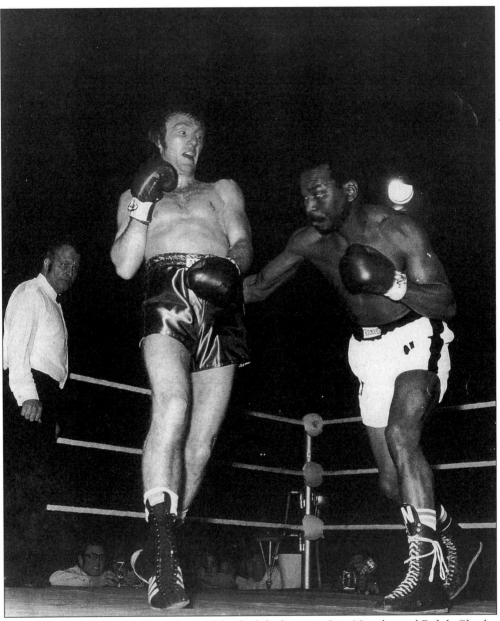

Jim Brimmell was the referee at this world title fight between Jose Napoles and Ralph Charles in 1972.

Jim Brimmell on the right pictured with Laszlo Papp (centre) and Tommy George, five times Welsh champion. Laszlo Papp was the only boxer to win three Olympic gold medals, and was visiting Cardiff as coach to an amateur boxing team. They are seen together at a farewell party in December 1973 at Grangetown Conservative Club.

Acknowledgements

I would like to thank the many people without whose advice, help and support this book could never have happened.

I am especially grateful to Dr Douglas A. Bassett and Mr A.V. (Vince) Jones (for their thoughtful and thorough reading of the proofs and many useful suggestions); Peter Farr; Tom Foster; Colin Jones (for access to the collection of the late Fred Jones and for other material); and Edith Shute.

Bill Barrett; S.A. Brain and Co. Ltd; Jim Brimmell; the Revd C. and Mrs Care (Porthcawl); Ian Clarke; G.A.C. (Geoff) Dart FLA; Professor M.J. Daunton; Christine Davies (Clydach Street Day Centre); Revd L.V. Davies; Michael Dunleavy; Joan Gallagher; Sidney Gilmore; David Goodchild; Grangetown Local History Society members; Olive Guppy; Dewi Jones; Professor Bernard Knight (for a splendid Foreword); Koda Press; Mr C. Langmaid; Sir James Lyons (thank you for your nostalgic reminiscences in the Introduction); The Welsh Industrial and Maritime Museum (National Museum of Wales); Captain Penny (Salvation Army); Peter Perkins; Mr J. O'Reilly; the Revd T. Glen Thomas; E. Turner & Sons Ltd; Bob Wheeler; Michael Wilcox; Muriel Williams; Stewart Williams (publisher of *Cardiff Yesterday*) and everyone who has contributed in any way at all to this publication.

This is not as complete a pictorial history of Grangetown as I would have ideally liked it to be. I have done my best to obtain as many photographs as possible and I hope now that this book will awaken further interest in the community's history. I will be delighted if more people come forward with photographs and contributions so that a second volume, in the not too distant future, might be a possibility.

I would also like to thank the staff of both Cardiff Central Library (Local History Section) and Grangetown Library for their help and advice, also to my editor, Simon Eckley, and the Chalford Publishing Company for their understanding and patience in waiting for this volume to be completed.

Finally, a word of thanks and tribute to the late Bryan Jones, a wise counsel for me in matters of local history. Without his inspiration and encouragement in the beginning I would never have embarked on this venture. His book, published last year, to which this is intended as a companion, will, however, remain for me a treasured reminder of his love and intelligent observation of all things Canton and Cardiff.